Special Praise for
A Man's Way through Relationships

"Dan Griffin is the authority on addressing men's issues in recovery. I highly recommend this book to all men who have been socialized in the 'Man Rules,' not just those who identify as being in recovery, in addition to recommending its value for us women who love them, and for any professional working with men. Dan's wisdom, writing style, and enlightened insight into twelve-step recovery blend harmoniously in this book, a major contribution to the field."

Jamie Marich, PhD, LPCC-S, LICDC-CS
Clinician and Creator of Dancing Mindfulness
Author of *Trauma and the Twelve Steps*, *EMDR Made Simple*, and *Trauma Made Simple*

"Dan Griffin has written a guide—from the heart—about the most challenging and ultimately rewarding task for men in our age: navigating the complex maze of intimate relationships. Written especially for men in recovery, his words and guidelines will be valuable for men of all backgrounds at any life stage."

David B. Wexler, PhD
Author of *When Good Men Behave Badly*

"A beautiful book about men and for men, *A Man's Way through Relationships* takes the reader through the journey of how the Man Rules, as part of socialization, often combine with trauma in early childhood to impact the ability of men to feel safe and embrace and flourish in relationships. I am a big fan of Dan Griffin and his contributions to treatment and recovery. This book is important to men in general, and specifically to men in recovery. Every man needs to read this!"

Claudia Black, PhD, Addiction and Trauma Specialist
Author of *It Will Never Happen to Me* and *Intimate Treason*

"Dan Griffin is a new sort of man, and he has written a new sort of book about men: honest and courageous, yet vulnerable and accessible. His perspective has been so thoroughly imbued with what he has learned about men from his experiences with men in recovery that his work fairly crackles with the immediacy of the men's lives. Relationships are a central part of these lives, no less—and no more—than they are for women. Dan's style is alternately authoritative and self-effacing, reflecting what he knows to be the case about male vulnerability: that it is only through this vulnerability, not around it, that men become 'all that they may be.'"

Roger D. Fallot, PhD
Director of Research and Evaluation
Community Connections

"Dan's insights and experience as they relate to men's need for love and wholeness through relationships are foundational to a meaningful and complete life. From both an experiential and theoretical perspective, the concepts are made accessible, while his passion for the process makes it compelling. The rawness is balanced with gentleness, while his honesty and courage inspire. Our struggle to overcome the isolation and pain inherent in abiding by the Man Rules is validated and the guidance through the process priceless."

Steven Millette
Executive Director, CeDAR
University of Colorado Hospital

"A stunning and important piece of work. The Man Rules we all grew up with simply don't serve us well—not in our relationships and not in our recovery. Dan examines vulnerability in the context of courage, and in so doing lays out a course to help guys like us navigate those relationships in our lives. The edgy beauty of Dan's work is that in the process of getting to know ourselves better as men, we will ultimately come to know ourselves as better men."

Bobby Ferguson
Founder and CEO
Jaywalker Lodge

A Man's Way through
Relationships

A Man's Way through
Relationships

Learning to Love
and Be Loved

DAN GRIFFIN

CENTRAL RECOVERY PRESS

Las Vegas

Central Recovery Press (CRP) is committed to publishing exceptional materials addressing addiction treatment, recovery, and behavioral healthcare topics, including original and quality books, audio/visual communications, and web-based new media. Through a diverse selection of titles, we seek to contribute a broad range of unique resources for professionals, recovering individuals and their families, and the general public.

For more information, visit www.centralrecoverypress.com.

Publisher: Central Recovery Press
            3321 N. Buffalo Drive
            Las Vegas, NV 89129

19 18 17 16   2 3 4 5

ISBN: 978-1-937612-66-5 (paper)
       978-1-937612-67-2 (e-book)

Author photo by Craig VanDerSchaegen. Used with permission.

Quotations from Jamie Marich, PhD, used with permission.

Quotations from Peter Levine used with permission.

Lyrics from Lynyrd Skynyrd's "Simple Man" reprinted with permission.

Publisher's Note: This book contains general information about relationships, recovery, and men's socialization and development. Central Recovery Press makes no representations or warranties in relation to the information herein; it is not an alternative to relationship, recovery, or medical advice from your behavioral heath professional or doctor or other professional healthcare provider.

Our books represent the experiences and opinions of their authors only. Every effort has been made to ensure that events, institutions, and statistics presented in our books as facts are accurate and up-to-date. To protect their privacy, some of the names of people, places, and institutions have been changed.

Cover design and interior design and layout by Deb Tremper

I dedicate this book to my beautiful daughter, Grace, and all of the boys and girls growing up today in a world so full of possibilities. May this be one more light to help show you the way as you experience the incredible joy and pain of learning how to love and be loved.

And to all of the men, like me, still living with the legacies of the Man Rules, who are struggling to connect and live fully in their relationships.

Table of Contents

FOREWORD

The addiction field has been slow in integrating gender-informed treatment. The early pioneers in this area argued that in order to produce better outcomes for women, the unique issues women faced in recovery needed to be incorporated into the therapeutic milieu. In the 1990s Dr. Terry Davis and Dr. Stephanie Covington were two names that stood out in creating female gender-informed treatment protocols. What happened next in recovery paralleled what happened in our society. The first focus of making treatment gender-informed for men emphasized helping men break the cycle of violence affecting families and communities. While a very necessary step, this unfortunately reinforced the stereotype of men as predators, bullies, and lacking in empathy. We were typecast as aggressive and obsessed with power. I am not denying that these are important issues to address in helping men, because they absolutely are; I am saying that we are much more than this. In fact, this focus was quite unfortunate because it stopped short and failed to address the plethora of other issues that men struggle with in accepting help and embracing recovery.

It wasn't until 2009 when Dan Griffin published *A Man's Way through the Twelve Steps* that we started to step back and really understand the experiences of men in recovery. This was a very important piece of work and eventually led Dan, Dr. Stephanie Covington, and Rick Dauer to develop the first trauma-informed protocol to help treatment programs become more aware of the issues that men encounter and struggle with in recovery. In this new book, Dan is now extending his work to focus on men's relationships.

When men in recovery open up their souls to other men, they grieve. They grieve the loss of a connection to their fathers and mothers, to their wives, to their siblings, and to their sons and daughters. They grieve the loss of a part of themselves that they could not integrate into the rigid gender rules for men. They grieve the loss of their ability to connect to those they love.

Relationships are an integral part of our psychological imperative to strive toward self-actualization. This basic need, as Abraham Maslow called it, is a powerful force in our lives that, when honored, moves us toward wholeness and maturation. Relationships are people growers. If we are honest with ourselves, and this is a big *if,* we will learn who we are and, even more importantly, who we aren't in our relationships. In order to do this we need to be willing to endure discomfort and learn to tolerate the feedback from our partners.

Our partners know us better than anyone else. They see who we are and who we aren't. Who we aren't creates trouble in our connections. Trouble does not mean there is something wrong with our relationship; quite the contrary. The trouble we encounter means that something is right. This is how relationships grow people. If we honestly face the trouble we are having in our relationships and remain open to seeing the next step in our emotional development, we will mature. We will grow up and learn how to be a better partner and support ourselves in the context of a committed relationship. Earnie Larsen called this Stage II Recovery. Dan and I call it emotional sobriety or emotional recovery.

I have heard many men say that they wish their relationship came with an instruction manual. Well, now you have one. *A Man's Way through Relationships: Learning to Love and Be Loved* will provide you with a map of the topography of relationships. Dan's message is that we cannot reach our full potential if we don't critically examine how the rules of manhood are affecting our lives. He encourages us to challenge ourselves and develop an awareness of these rules so we can actually choose the man we want to be. But Dan doesn't just preach this message; he shows us the value of this approach by sharing with us his own struggles openly and honestly. I was inspired by his vulnerability, his insight, and his willingness to share those things that most men won't dare discuss.

What I love about this book is that Dan speaks to us like we are sitting with him at Starbucks and having a cup of coffee. He doesn't come off as the all-knowing professional, but rather as a fellow traveler who is sharing with us what he has learned along his journey. Men help men become better men, and if you let him, Dan will guide you to become a better partner, a better father, a better friend, and a better son. This is an important book, and not just for men in recovery. I encourage you to read it, do the exercises, and share what you learn with those you love.

Allen Berger, PhD, Clinical Psychologist
Author of *Love Secrets Revealed, 12 Stupid Things That Mess Up Recovery, 12 Smart Things to Do When the Booze and Drugs Are Gone,* and *12 Hidden Rewards of Making Amends*

ACKNOWLEDGMENTS

Very special thanks to Rick Dauer, with whom I have shared much of this journey the past four years, who has taught me a lot and helped me expound on a lot of these concepts, and whose support in writing and editing this book has been invaluable. Thank you, Rick.

Thank you to Stephanie Covington for helping to open the doors for this message.

Special thanks to my good friend, colleague, and mentor, Dr. Allen Berger, for taking the time to read through my drafts and offer me invaluable feedback.

Thank you to all my family: the Griffins, the Dietls, and the Robsons. Love and thanks to my mom, Sherry Griffin, for everything. All of my love and gratitude to Nancy and Grace for helping me every day to become a better man, a better husband, and a better father.

Many thanks to Central Recovery Press for having the courage to declare the importance of this topic by publishing *A Man's Way through Relationships,* for having faith in me, and for not kowtowing to the old belief that men don't buy books about relationships! Thanks also to Hazelden for publishing my first book, *A Man's Way through the Twelve Steps*. I have absolutely no evidence from the work I have been doing nationally and internationally that this work does not resonate with men. That is what it is going to take to effect the change that so many men truly desire to have in their lives.

Thanks to Dan Mager for making the editing process, which can be as painful as the writing, a wonderful example of how men can collaborate and work through conflict.

Finally, very special and heartfelt thanks to all the men who shared themselves and their truths with me to help me create this book: for your time, your vulnerability, your trust, and the incredible work you have done to become the men you are in this world. I hope your act of service will make a difference in the lives of men for years to come.

INTRODUCTION

Where the Hell Am I Going and How the Hell Do I Get There?

I was recently in London and had the opportunity to visit the underground bunkers used by Winston Churchill and his staff during World War II. While London was under siege, they strategized the defeat of Adolf Hitler and the Nazi regime from these secure and incredibly well-fortified dwellings, known as the War Rooms. Throughout these bunkers were maps. Many of the maps showed the locations of the different battleship groups around the world, those of both the enemy and the Allies, tracking their movement. What would they have done without these maps? They would not have been able to see the more complete picture. Not only did the maps show the layout of the current situation, they also helped the British think about and plan their next moves and develop a vision of where they wanted to end up. The strategy for winning the war was contingent on having the context and information these maps provided.

So, where are the maps for men in recovery in our quest to love and be loved? They are few and far between. Maps for women? Yes, some wonderful ones. Maps for couples? Yes, many. But maps written just for men and written by men, especially for those in recovery from addiction? Not really. Why? There is a long-standing belief that men don't care about relationships as much as women do. The good thing is that we are not at war in our relationships. It is not a battle and should not feel like one, even though for many men I know it does. As men we attempt this journey, often with little idea of where we are going. We try to steer our ships on the treacherous seas of intimacy, vulnerability, trust, and love, often crashing on the rocks of our belief systems about men. These rocks are everywhere, and if we are not paying attention, they will sink every meaningful relationship we set foot in.

We all know that men don't often ask for directions, even when they are lost, but they might just use a map. This book is meant to provide such a map—one that can help chart some of the territory that has yet to be crossed successfully. Just for men. Just for you. Of course, a map is of little value unless it is used.

In my first book, *A Man's Way through the Twelve Steps,* I wrote about important areas that have been poorly addressed in men's treatment and recovery. Men and women thank me for having the courage to take on the toughest aspects of men's recovery. As in that first book, some of the information contained here has been gathered through interviews with men I respect and admire, many of whom have been on the journey of recovery much longer than I. I interviewed over thirty men: gay and straight; older and younger; men of diverse ethnic, racial, socioeconomic, and spiritual/religious (including the nonreligious) backgrounds. Each of these men had at least ten years in recovery, and many of them had twenty-plus years. A few men even had over thirty-five years in recovery. All of them trusted me enough to be willing to be open and vulnerable in their responses. And the similarities across so many of their responses were striking.

Do Men Care About Relationships?

Bobby, one of the men I interviewed for this book, said it well: "Life is meaningful only within the context of the connections we have with the friends and family around us." I have always cared about the relationships in my life. My guess is that you have, too. I did not always know how to show it, or have the courage to show it, and I would often act in ways that sent the message that I didn't care. I had no map. I did not know how to navigate the terrain. Relationships are complicated and challenging territory for everyone, but particularly for men. Even today, relationships can sometimes leave me wishing I lived on a deserted island, just as they did when I was stuck in my active addiction. I still don't always know, or have the courage to show, how much I care about the relationships in my life. I certainly do not do it perfectly.

The assumption that underlies this book is that all men care about relationships. We want to be good sons, partners/spouses, fathers, and friends, but we need help. We are shaped by these "Rules" about being males that tell us asking for help is not okay. We may follow these Rules, but they belie what is in our hearts. I have worked with, sat with, cried with, and even physically held far too many men to ever believe that deep inside of most men's hearts is not a real desire to connect, to love, and to be loved. Yet, an incredible force inside of them pushes them to separate, disconnect, push away, and pretend otherwise. This seeming contradiction is at the heart of this book and the conversation in which I want to engage you.

The process of recovery and the Twelve Steps embodies some of the greatest tools to help us find our way in relationships. This book is for all men, but focuses specifically on men in recovery. It is another tool you can put in your toolbox to help you become more successful in all of your relationships. As Mark, another of the men I interviewed for this book, said, "Without recovery, I have no relationships." And I would argue that without relationships, there is no quality life for any of us. This book can help you find your way when you feel lost—and you will get lost. To effectively use it, though, a real man will first have to find the courage to admit that he is lost. Then, he will have to be open to experimenting with new ideas and new behaviors that offer the possibility of finding his way back to the path toward healthy relationships.

A lot of us feel as though we were absent the day they passed out the manual on relationships in school. There is beauty in learning that we need to depend on others if we want to make real progress and that we must dig deep and take risks to go outside of our comfort zone. It requires us to humble ourselves again and again, admitting to ourselves and others that we are confused. We are lost. We are scared. We are angry. We are hurt. We are insecure. Previously, we hid all this underneath our armor of beliefs about how men are supposed to be. In this journey through life, we succeed by taking off the armor.

Any man who seeks to participate fully in his relationships will experience failure. That failure may look different for different men, but we cannot succeed without risking failure. Out of that failure comes our liberation and the transformation of our relationships as we become fully known to others. As counterintuitive as it seems, invite that failure into your life. Embrace it. Failing means you are trying and pushing yourself. It means you are being courageous in the face of fear.

To what extent do you feel encouraged to engage in your relationships? I do not mean guilt-tripped or manipulated, or any of the actions you may have taken due to a feeling of obligation. I mean *encouraged*. If women want men to step up in relationships, they need to encourage us and see us as partners rather than as large children. And men have to stop being passive about their participation in relationships and stop acting like children, especially when their partners need them to be serious adults. As my wife, Nancy, says, "I need my grown-up husband right now." Time to put on those big-boy pants.

Those men who truly care about and want to improve how men are viewed in the context of relationships need to speak up because there are too many men acting out the most damaging parts of the masculine script, giving women and others every reason to believe the worst about them. They take the more stereotypical macho path and typically hurt a lot of people along the way, including themselves. Yet, even most of the guys we consider "jerks," "cretins," "playas," and "douche bags" want more out of their relationships and want to be more within them—they simply do not know how to get there. They are confused, unsure, and scared. They are acting like boys. They are following the "Man Rules" to a tee. They want love and connection, but they don't have a map. They are simply adrift.

The Journey

Learning to love and be loved is the greatest journey you will take. If you are reading this book, you have already begun or are ready to begin this journey. But this journey is different from most of the others we have taken as men, where the armor of self-protection may have had a useful purpose. As I stated earlier, we need to take off the armor in order to make progress. We think the armor protects us, but instead it separates us from others. In the process, it kills love—sometimes quickly, sometimes slowly, but almost inevitably.

This journey takes place mostly inside us. As men are expected to be more engaged, more emotionally present, more everything in our relationships, most of us are (or were) floundering in trying to do it on our own. In the world of twelve-step recovery, we have been given permission to seek help when we need it. Recovery teaches us Emotions 101—how to feel our emotions and express them in healthy ways, a prerequisite for success in any relationship. Recovery also teaches us how to think of someone other than ourselves and how to be a part of the community, two other prerequisites. Recovery is the perfect training ground for men to learn new ways to act and be in relationships with others.

We spend every moment of our day in and out of relationships. You say all you do is work? Guess what? With few exceptions, work is all about relationships—with every person you pass, every person you email or text, every person you call, every person you convince yourself is the reason you are having a bad day, and every person you stand with in silence on the elevator. And when you are sitting in your office with the door closed, staring at the computer screen like a zombie, you are still immersed in a relationship. With whom? Well, with the most important person in your life—you.

Based on my interviews with men for this book, there appear to be no significant differences between what gay and heterosexual men value and struggle with in their relationships. In fact, while a lot of the language in this book may seem to be focused only on heterosexual relationships, I have worked hard to make it applicable to all men. There seems to be a common thread, regardless of sexual orientation, race, ethnicity, age, and other variables—that is, the challenges we share in a world full of expectations and Rules that make it hard to feel "like a man," to feel good about ourselves, and to be our best in our relationships. Though we may experience these challenges somewhat differently as individuals, some groups of men experience them differently from others, and some groups (such as gay men or men of color) may have unique challenges;

my focus is on the common struggle of men to connect with others in ways that are authentic and emotionally intimate.

That said, I know the importance for me to recognize the lens through which I see the world: I am a white, middle-class, heterosexual male of primarily Irish (and Polish and German) descent in recovery from alcohol and other drugs since May of 1994. I am a trauma survivor who has done and continues to do extensive work to heal from the pain of my experience, healing work that includes having had a father who was addicted to alcohol and who behaved violently. But it has clearly affected my relationships with other men and women and my perception of myself as a man. Another significant part of my trauma that I discuss in more detail throughout the book is having had to receive medical intervention to grow and achieve puberty over the course of six months at the end of my sophomore year of high school and through that following summer. This gave me a fairly unique view of the process of becoming a man. I also have a master's degree and trained to be an addiction counselor at one of the most prestigious addiction treatment facilities in the country and have worked in the addiction field for almost two decades. I have been married for over a decade to my beautiful wife Nancy, and we have an amazing daughter named Grace.

I believe, and the men I interviewed have convinced me, that a lot of these relationship issues transcend race, class, generations, and sexual orientation. That does not mean we are all the same. Some of these issues will apply directly to you and others will not. You are going to hear from men who have had incredible journeys in their relationships, some of whom have been married for decades. Others have experienced the pain of divorce or the death of a spouse. You may be surprised at the depth of the sharing and the honesty of those interviewed. The men in this book talk candidly about being fathers, lovers, friends, and men. They have learned hard-fought lessons about relationships, many through the high cost of pain.

We have all made plenty of mistakes in conducting our relationships. The point is that relationships take work. It may well be some of the toughest work you have ever done in your recovery, possibly your life. I have seen many men who have conquered incredible challenges brought to their knees by the struggles they faced in their relationships.

I also want to make one thing very clear: This is not a book that tells men how much they have screwed up relationships, or what assholes men are. Far from it. I was meeting with a group of men in recovery, and one with several decades of recovery said to me, "I sure hope you are going to talk about all of the things we do well. There are a lot of things we do that work and that should be celebrated." I could not agree more, and I hope that also comes through clearly in this book.

The Space Where We Meet

Men and women are not from different planets; we are, at most, from different countries, and we can teach each other our native language. I like to say that men are from Minnesota and women are from Wisconsin. We have a river that separates us, but we can always cross that river.

As a generalization, men and women have different relationship needs and skills. Women are not the only ones with the answers, contrary to what some think or espouse. As my wife Nancy says, each of us has to weed our own garden. That is, when relationships go well, both partners, irrespective of gender, are paying attention to their own side of the street, to their own "stuff." Both partners need to do the actual weeding, and get help from others when the weeds prove too numerous and/or deep-rooted. Relationships simply don't work when only one partner works to till and care for his or her garden. One of the last things that my mentor, Earnie Larsen, a phenomenal man who gave so much to our experience as people in recovery, told me shortly before he died, "Dan, I have become convinced that the only way any relationship can survive is if both partners are willing to do their work. Period."

There is a beautiful place where men and their partners meet in a relationship. It is at this place where both individuals are truly in a new space. Both have entered foreign territory; both have the opportunity to create and explore together a vast landscape of intimacy. Nancy and I hit this point several years ago, and it seems we keep hitting it at a deeper level after a decade of being married. It was here initially that we acknowledged we *both* did not know what we were doing. We both had to acknowledge that true intimacy and vulnerability are scary as hell. And that was okay. We have built our intimacy over the years and continue to do so. I cannot emphasize enough the importance of working through pain, grief, rejection, anger, and toxic shame as part of that process.

Consider men in recovery. Whether we are dressed in suits, biker gang attire, shorts and a T-shirt, or any other of the numerous skins we wear, you will most likely be amazed at what you hear us talking about—if you pay attention. You will hear men engaged in their relationships, working to understand their emotional lives, willing to see their role in problems, learning to be aware of their own needs and how to set boundaries. This is a sacred journey, and I want to encourage and celebrate the reality that it is possible for men to learn how to "do" relationships well without forfeiting their masculinity. I want to help those of you who, for fear of being vulnerable, have been unable to take off the armor that prevents you from being yourself and speaking your truth within your relationships. I want you to be one of those people who dares celebrate how wonderful men are. With all of our contradictions, imperfections, immaturity, and goofiness, we are still awesome. You are awesome. You may feel hopeless at times about your relationships. You may feel lost. But you can find your way with the help of others and a good map, such as this book.

Men Learn by Doing

In my many years of experience working with men, training others how to work more effectively with men, and in my own personal growth, it has become clear that many men learn by doing. We can read the ideas and even agree with them. But in order for many of us to truly learn it (whatever "it" is), we have to practice it. For that reason there are sections throughout the book with suggested assignments. I recommend that you buy a notebook specifically for completing the assignments. These are called "Into Action" and offer ways to practice applying the concepts and lessons in each chapter and sharing what you find with those closest to you.

It took many years to get this book published, because there is a prevailing myth out there that men will not read a book about relationships. The fact that you're reading these words proves that "they" are wrong. Men are not as predictable, stubborn, or one-dimensional as many would believe. I have known that for years now. So have many other men—and women. Now it's time to make sure that every man, both in and outside recovery, gets the same chance at having loving, quality, and healthy relationships. You deserve them. And everyone who loves you deserves to have them, too.

CHAPTER ONE

The Man Rules

"Recovery has allowed me to question the measures of manhood I had set for myself." –Jim

Has it ever felt to you like you were following some set of unwritten rules on how to be a man? Men can do *this* but can't do *that*. These are the Man Rules I referred to in the Introduction. They are unwritten yet very real, and they guide our lives from an early age, telling us how to be boys and men. We follow these Rules to let the world know that we are real boys and real men. When we don't follow them we run the risk of being viewed by others and viewing ourselves as being less than *real* boys or men. Where did the Rules come from? The answer is that they come from many different sources, some personal and some societal. The Rules come from both of our parents and other caregivers, from other family members, from coaches and teachers, from the kids on the playground, and from the media based on the images of "real" men presented on television, in movies, and in print and broadcast advertising. Adolescence can be a particularly brutal period of indoctrination to the Man Rules.

Think about your day-to-day experiences and look at how many Man Rules you follow. Think about how you may judge yourself as less than manly if you don't follow them. There is the Rule that real men do not ask for help. This rule contributes to many men remaining lost for much longer than necessary, among other problems. You may be pretty good at asking for help, but how do you feel when you do it? It's still hard for me to ask for help, and when I do it is frequently accompanied by some sort of self-criticism. If you are anything like me, every time you ask for help it is a struggle just to get to that point, and once there you probably have at least a twinge of shame around feeling or appearing weak or incompetent or stupid. But with time and practice, it gets better. Luke spoke for a lot of the men in recovery whom I know: "I had a huge amount of self-hatred before recovery, due to the nature of my acting out and hiding my true self from others. I had issues and doubts of myself about even being a man. Since recovery, the self-hatred has been greatly reduced, and I'm more confident in my masculinity and how I express it out in the world."

Some of the most common Man Rules I hear about from men *and* women are:

- Don't be weak.
- Don't show emotion.
- Don't ask for help.
- Don't cry.
- Don't care about relationships.

Do these sound familiar?

Into Action

▶ Take some time right now to write down as many Rules about being a man as you can think of. Think about the Rules you learned from your parents/caregivers, school, neighborhood/community, the media, and workplace. If you are having trouble, think of them in the following areas: Self, Relationships, Activities, Power, Sexuality, and Spirituality.

▶ Think of Rules that reinforce a healthier idea of masculinity. While the majority of the Rules are neither inherently bad nor good, how they tend to be enforced can be rigid and restricting. However, there are Man Rules like integrity and self-discipline that seem to be inherently healthy traits.

What does your list of Man Rules look like? My guess, if your experience is anything like the majority of the men and women I work with, is that you have not previously spent a lot of time consciously thinking about and attempting to identify these Rules.

Think about what you learned in elementary school of how Europeans imagined the New World (the Americas) looked before they actually had traversed the territory and were able to map it out. In some ways, those are just like the maps men have been using to navigate their way in relationships—out-of-date and inaccurate. The available maps for men are guided by the Man Rules. Like those who sought to explore the New World in the late fifteenth and early sixteenth centuries, we may imagine monsters lurking in the oceans and dangerous creatures dominating the land, along with the possibility of falling off the edge of the Earth. We have no real idea of what the landscape actually looks like. And, as the first explorers discovered in traveling previously uncharted territory, the risks were great, but so were the rewards. Yet the only way to learn this was to take the journey and face the many challenges and struggles along the way. Welcome to the new world of healthy relationships.

There is a story of two fish swimming in the ocean when a third fish swims up to them and says, "Hello, gents. How's the water?" and he swims away. The two fish look at each other and say, "What the hell is water?" In this way, the Water becomes a metaphor for those built-in aspects of our experience we take for granted to such an extent that we don't even notice them. That is how the Rules show up in so many of our lives. We have no awareness of them; we do not see them because we are so used to them being there as a natural part of our experience. We react to them as if they are the only version of reality—the one truth. However, they are social constructions that have been created by other men (and women) and passed on. Most of us were never given a choice. Nobody sat us down, reviewed the Rules with us, and asked us which ones we wanted to follow and which ones didn't fit for us. In all likelihood we became immersed in them early in our lives when we were incapable of thinking about them critically. We never had the opportunity to consider whether the Rules made sense for who we were and who we wanted to become.

When I walked into my first recovery meeting a man tried to hug me as a welcoming gesture. Another man, named Bud, wearing a sweat-covered T-shirt and a "Honk if you Love Tits" baseball cap, was one of the first men I noticed standing around. Twenty minutes later this same man—one I arrogantly thought embodied so much of what I detested about traditional masculinity—was crying as he talked about his marriage falling apart at seven years of recovery and how he had been kicked out of the house again.

"Whoa. What is going on here?" I asked myself. And that was the first time I began to see the Water. I realized right away that in the rooms of the twelve-step community men expressed themselves differently than they did virtually everywhere else in our society (though that has changed somewhat during the past two decades).

Of course, that was one of many examples from my first year of recovery that I could point to demonstrating how men in twelve-step recovery tend to express masculinity differently than in American society at-large. The more I travel the country talking about these issues, the clearer it is that the biggest problem with the Man Rules is how oblivious to them so many of us are.

This is what Jim is talking about in the quote that heads this chapter; he has a choice now in how he gets to be a man and what that means to him. He is becoming aware of the Water. The freedom inherent in this idea is immeasurable, yet so many men have no idea of the opportunities and choices that are available to them. A lot of men have not thought about their ideas of being a man. If you do not consciously reflect on this, you can't see or feel the Water in which you are swimming. When asked about the process of how his ideas of being a man have evolved, Jose said it this way: "I've let go of old ideas that I thought served me well but were actually based on false information or poor perspective on my part."

How aware of your own internal conversations are you? What do the voices from your past tell you about being a man? I encourage you to listen closely without preconceptions. Only in this way can you come to truly see the Water in which you swim every day.

My guess is that a lot of the Rules have been invisible to you. If we do not consciously call them out, they tend to operate in the shadows, driving a lot of our behavior, with little awareness on our part. We treat them as reality, and as inevitable. How often have you heard the dismissive phrase, "Well, that's just how men are"? I have heard it all of my life, and a lot of the time it did not apply to me. So I thought the only thing that made sense to me at the time was, *I must not be much of a man.* That sentiment haunted me for a long time, and I didn't think I could tell anyone about it. Once I had the courage to begin talking about the insecurity of feeling like I wasn't a real man and share about the negative judgments I hurled at myself, I heard from man after man that I was not alone; many men have these feelings in common.

Let me be very clear that the Rules are not necessarily bad. How the Rules are taught to us (sometimes literally beaten into us) and how we respond to them can be problematic. Rigidly following the Rules is unhealthy because there is no freedom; there is no choice. The Rules at their extremes are toxic. They lead to disconnection, violence, homophobia, objectification of women, and extreme competition, as well as isolation, loneliness, self-hatred, and misery. Discover who you are despite the Rules, and you cannot help but become the man you were meant to be. With self-aware practice, the Rules become more relaxed and flexible. They feel less like tight, constricting clothes and more like loose-fitting, comfortable garments. Mike said this about how recovery and the Twelve Steps had changed his ideas of who he was as a man: "I like what I see when I look in the mirror. I have come to a level of self-acceptance I'm comfortable with."

Many of the men (and women) I know who defend their behavior by saying, "It's just who I am," are often lost in the Rules because they are not aware of the Water. These are the people who keep using old, out-of-date maps. It is easier to simply say men don't know how to communicate feelings and continue to be disconnected in their relationships than to take the risk of communicating feelings. That involves immense vulnerability for those of us who have been told all of our lives that sharing feelings, outside of anger, is not manly. As Mike says, "When I share my feelings, honest connection is possible." The converse also seems to be true: When we do not share our feelings or our inner lives, it is hard to truly connect with others. This is just one of the many "ways that men are" that I still hear all the time, even in the rooms of recovery.

Of course, the Rules are not always specific and concrete; they can be a set of ideas that we react to or resist. For instance, all of my life I have felt more emotional and sensitive than most men (and women). I have found this to be a common trait I share with a lot of men in recovery. The Rules, however, dictate that men are not to show emotions other than anger, and that certain emotions, such as fear, sadness, and hurt, are signs of weakness. These emotions are associated with being feminine, which in the context of the Man Rules has negative connotations. Maybe we feel "less than." We may even spend a fair amount of time trying not to engage in certain Rules that we consider unhealthy and even destructive, but doing so may affect how we feel about ourselves as men. However, if we're self-aware and allow ourselves to experience how becoming emotionally vulnerable can enhance the quality of our connections with others, through practice we begin to have a better understanding of the man we want to be rather than one whose relationships are being suffocated by the Rules.

Implicit in many of the Rules are a lot of "don'ts." For example, if the Rule is "Men have to be strong," an underlying message is "Don't be weak." Which is the greater Rule—that men have to be strong or that men cannot be weak or show weakness of any kind? In other words, the negatives associated with many of the Rules tend to be the stronger part of the message. These "don'ts" are important because, at the heart of it, they are telling us as men what and who *not to be*. How much of your identity is built around what and who you *are not*? How much time do you spend *not being* somebody as opposed to *being someone,* or more importantly, being *who you are* and *who you want to become?*

Interestingly, if you look at the "don'ts" and get rid of the word "don't," you get a list of Rules that tend to be associated with a particular group of people. Let's look at some of them.

- ~~Don't~~ be weak.
- ~~Don't~~ show emotion.
- ~~Don't~~ ask for help.

- ~~Don't~~ cry.
- ~~Don't~~ care about relationships.

What group do we tend to identify these statements with? Women. Practically from the moment we are born, men are raised with messages that conflict with those given to girls and women. We receive messages— explicitly and implicitly—that not only are certain behaviors against the Rules, they are to be avoided because they are associated with the "weaker" sex. Now, consider that some of the same behaviors are exactly what we are expected to practice in our most intimate relationships. This is one of the phenomena that creates serious internal tension for men and conflict between men and women in relationships.

You may be saying, "But, Dan, I don't live by a lot of these Rules." Fair enough. But as a man you are still frequently judged consistent with them. Chances are there is still a voice inside you, a model of a "manly" man that you have internalized, with a tendency to judge you more harshly than you realize when you don't follow the Rules. I know that is the case for me, and I have been living an examined life with respect to my masculinity for a very long time.

The Man Rules have also changed a lot in the past two decades. They have loosened up, allowing for what I referred to in my master's research as a "relaxed masculinity." The armor I talked about earlier is less rigid. We have more flexibility and more room in which to move. I am convinced we are on the right path as we evolve as individual human beings and as a society. Unfortunately, I have also found that this relaxed masculinity can cause a great deal of confusion. In the 1940s, 1950s, and early 1960s the Rules were pretty clear. Men and women knew exactly how to act and how to be in relationship with each other. Half a century later there is much less clarity and certainty. Under what circumstances is it okay to show weakness? When is it acceptable and preferable to be vulnerable with our authentic emotions? Some men have learned the hard way that when they do not follow the Rules they are made fun of or rejected for not being manly enough, not only by men in their lives, but by women as well. Understandably, women can buy into the Man Rules as much as men do. They don't see the Water either.

The Rules provide one very important experience for all men: safety. When I ask audiences what following the Man Rules offers men, they often say "acceptance" or "sense of belonging." I will push them to look further underneath that. What does acceptance, a sense of belonging, or being liked give us? Safety. At the heart of the Rules is an attempt to be safe in the world, to not only be validated as men but to truly feel safe and fit in. Every young boy learns that when he follows the Man Rules he is safer in that he is less likely to be made fun of, criticized, beaten up, and so on. The majority of us did not learn the Rules in peaceful conditions. Maybe your home had a more enlightened approach to gender, but no boy escapes the brutality of the schoolyard. In fact, I would say that given how much the process of socialization cuts us off from core parts of our humanity, there is a degree of trauma experienced by every man. For some of us the trauma is severe. To make matters worse, at the heart of any attempts we make to be intimate and truly known to others is a level of vulnerability that we may not be prepared for or have the ability to navigate. This experience can touch our trauma, triggering it constantly in our most intimate relationships, and when it happens we have no idea what to do and end up sabotaging our relationships as a result.

Finally, there is another nuance of the Rules that affects some men differently than others that must not be ignored. The people I have had the honor to train and share this conversation with have helped me to see more of the Water. When we think of criminals or drug dealers, whose face do we tend to see? When we think of illegal immigrants or people doing menial work, if they are even men, whose faces do we see? The point is that the Man Rules are not color-blind or classless. I will never know what it is like to walk down the street and have people fearing me simply because of the color of my skin. Or make judgments about me and my intelligence, moral character, or basic humanity simply because of the color of my skin or who I am drawn to love. The intensity and expression of the Man Rules also seem to be different in the suburbs where I grew up than they are in the inner city, the child protection system, or the juvenile and criminal justice systems. All men are not socialized equally.

Through the process of recovery, something happens to us that changes how we express ourselves at the foundation of our identity: our gender. Many people can get confused about the difference between sex and gender, not to mention sexuality (covered later in this book). Our sex is a biological and physiological attribute based upon having specific genitalia and other key distinguishing factors (breasts, etc.), even though there is much variation among human beings, even physiologically. Gender, however, is a social construct. It varies according to so many things and is a fluid concept. What masculinity means in one country versus another can be very different. How we express our gender is malleable and often changes over time and even through the course of relationships.

Many of us are unaware of what happens to our gender in recovery and personal growth because it occurs in the context of our recovery, as part of a bigger process of learning and growth. That was certainly what I found when I interviewed men over fifteen years ago for my master's research, as well as among the men I interviewed for *A Man's Way through the Twelve Steps*. When I asked, "How have your ideas of being a man changed since getting into recovery?" the number-one answer was "They haven't." I followed up with "You mean before recovery you walked around hugging other men? Asking for help? Talking about your feelings?" It was only when these changes were pointed out and they began to reflect on the question that they saw they were very different from the men they were before recovery. The same thing happened with a number of the men I interviewed for this book.

Men and women are essentially raised to be half human beings: Women are given one part and men the other. The breakdown could look like this:

Feminine	Socialization Process	Masculine
Emotional Intelligence (EQ)	Intellect	Logical Intelligence (IQ)
Retreat/Isolation/Internalization	Response to Trauma	Aggression/Externalization
Collaboration/Decentralized	Power	Control/Hierarchy
Process/Intuition	Information	Analytical/Rational
Relational	Self-Development	Individual
Surrender/Intimacy	Sex/Love	Conquest/Performance
Codependence	Relationships	Independence

We hear from an early age that "boys don't do *that*" and "girls don't do *that*." Case in point: I was visiting my sister a few years ago. I was wearing a necklace made of different-colored, small, rounded stones. When my two-year-old nephew saw it he said, as intelligibly as he could, "Why are you wearing that?" "What?" I said. "That necklace. Boys don't wear necklaces," he said with great seriousness. I laughed, and yet I thought to myself, *holy sh%$! Seriously? That young?* My daughter also does this all the time. She doesn't hear it from me, but she still "knows" that boys don't paint their fingernails or wear long hair. It is not at all uncommon for her to make comments like "Boys don't do . . ." and "Girls don't do . . . ." These are observations she is making about the world in which she lives, and if I do not challenge those comments they become fact for her, stored in the processor of her brain. It becomes part of her Water, with no awareness on her part that it is happening. It happened to me, and it happened to you.

There Is No Gender Neutral

Without breaking into a treatise on oppression and marginalization, we cannot ignore the reality that some people receive benefits and advantages in this society simply because they belong to a certain category. And others get just the opposite—deficits and disadvantages—because they belong to another category or, said another way, do not belong to the dominant group. In terms of gender, men are the dominant group in our society (as in many others). Our society is patriarchal and "maleness" is the norm, the expectation, and even the subconscious default for many men and women. Unless both men and women are aware of this, it infiltrates all of our relationships in insidious ways. Once we are aware of it, we can choose to transcend it.

The issue of gender becomes even more complicated when you consider gay men or men of color who are part of a dominant group (men) and also members of a minority or marginalized group. As Gary put it in *A Man's Way through the Twelve Steps,* "Even though I am a man, I am a gay man, and being a gay man is the worst of both worlds. I am seen as a predator, weak, dangerous, sick, and as the 'other' all at once by the same people." Psychologically, this can have seriously damaging effects on how these men express their masculinity and how they are able to engage in their relationships.

As we adhere to the old adage "To thine own self be true," we begin to move toward wholeness as individuals. We round out the rough edges of our character and discover our true selves. The more we engage in our recovery and the process of personal growth, the more likely we are to move toward authentically expressing who we are. One aspect of this process is learning to love parts of ourselves that we were taught or told were not okay. Another aspect is coming to embrace parts of ourselves that we rejected. A third aspect is expanding what we see as possible, including ways of being that we never considered or had rejected without ever exploring, often because "boys (or girls) don't act that way." As I stated earlier, as a young boy I was always sensitive. I learned very early growing up in a violent alcoholic home that being sensitive was not okay (or emotionally safe). I learned to fear and hate that part of myself because I thought it was not manly. I have come to realize that it is a central part of who I am and I do not care if others think it is manly or not. In fact, it is a wonderful quality when I choose to express it in a healthy way.

Chances are you have your own examples of similar experiences. What is important is to be able to verbalize those experiences in a safe environment. This requires doing the work of self-examination and self-discovery. Equally important, however, is that you look at your experiences through the lens of gender to help the unseen become seen.

On a spiritual and moral plane, we don't ever prosper by treating others as inferior or second class, or by engaging in any of the other ways human beings disparage one another. Nor do we ever prosper by accepting such statements. Such actions affect our spirit deeply. This is particularly true for those of us in recovery, because we are not dulling our consciousness or conscience. We are aware, are living an examined life, and are challenged to see that other people are not responsible for our behavior. And we become aware that the differences between individuals do not confer a status of one person as "better than" another. In fact, the differences enrich our lives. Ultimately, the two primary questions for men that I pose are: How are your behaviors consistent with the man the people in your life truly want you to be? More importantly, how are your behaviors and the beliefs you maintain reflective of the man you want to be?

If you want to have loving and fulfilling relationships, I cannot stress this enough: Screw the Rules! Be who you are, and you cannot help but show up, authentically and as the best man you could ever be. As Jim said in the quote at the beginning of this chapter, recovery gives you the opportunity to redefine what a man is and what that looks like for you. Bob said it this way: "My history of male models has lots of bravado, independence, and low emotional expressiveness. Since recovery I have been more willing to allow interdependence and emotional expressivity as essential aspects of me. As a result, I am more comfortable in my own skin."

Into Action

- ▸ Take your own list of Rules and share them with your spouse, partner, and/or sponsor. Have a conversation with them about your Rules.

- ▸ Consciously look at the Rules you have listed. Which ones do you want to keep? Which ones would you like to get rid of? Which ones would you like to change?

- ▸ Choose three Rules you want to keep and write about how they have helped you and your relationships. Share what you have written with your partner or a trusted friend.

- ▸ Choose three Rules that you want to let go of or change and write about how they have hurt you and your relationships. Share what you have written with your partner or a trusted friend.

- ▸ What are five behaviors or interests you have that would be considered less masculine? What is it like for you to admit that? How long have you had those behaviors or interests? How were you treated when you exhibited them?

CHAPTER TWO
My Story

If someone is taking you on a journey, you probably want to have some confidence that that person knows where he or she is going. If you are going to follow that person, you may want to know a little more about him or her. Well, I am going to do my best to be a guide, so I would like to share a little more about myself and what this journey has been like for me.

Like a lot of men, I was not given a very good map with which to chart the course of my life and my relationships. I do not blame anyone *anymore* for that; it is just how it worked out. My parents didn't have very good maps, either. I have tried to map out the specific landscape of my relationships and have a better sense of where I am headed. Metaphorically, I have spent a lot of my life wanting to get to Paris, France, not realizing that my map only took me to Paris, Texas! The relationships I have craved in my life have been there, but I did not know how to find them—or appreciate them when I did. And again, this struggle starts with the Rules.

Every man has his own relationship to the Man Rules. I was born in 1972. If there were one word that would best describe the way my generation (and subsequent generations) responds to the Rules, it would be *confusion*. For many of us, the Rules (though still in effect and still invisible) have been softened and have become less stringent than they were in previous generations. That is both positive and negative. It is positive because we have more room to move around as far as what is expected of us. It is negative, however, because there is less certainty. There is more flexibility, but it is less clear when a particular Rule is going to be enforced and when it is not.

I was a rough-and-tumble kid. I was very athletic. I loved to play football with the neighborhood kids, and I was good at it. But Mom wouldn't let me play football out of fear I would get hurt. I played soccer and excelled at that, along with street hockey, BMX, tennis, and golf. I loved playing with soldiers and matchbox cars, and doing anything outside. I was a boy's boy. But I did not consider myself tough. As I mentioned earlier, I was also very sensitive and emotional. I seemed to have an inborn anxiety. This was all one big strike against me; it was against the Rules. I was the kid who would tackle another boy and feel bad if I hurt him. I hated violence. I didn't like to fight. Strike two: I was a mama's boy. She was the one I attached to and spent a lot of time protecting and trying to comfort when my father hurt her both emotionally and physically. I cried a lot. I also liked to read, write poetry, and even play with my sister and her friends. More strikes against me. More violations of the Rules. Nonetheless, on the surface I was pretty much following the same map as the rest of my friends. Though I was considered popular, and even "cool," internally I felt confused and conflicted.

As an adolescent I had an unusual and deeply painful experience. My body literally did not grow. To say I was a late bloomer is an understatement. I became acutely aware of this in eighth grade, but there were still a few other boys who also had yet to hit puberty. The summer between eighth and ninth grade I had hoped "it" would happen, but it didn't. I stayed short and began to feel more and more powerless. The shame about who I was and about my body began to spread like a weed throughout my psyche. It was a secret, and I had to protect myself from being found out to save myself from the ultimate humiliation.

I was five feet tall and about ninety pounds when I entered high school. I was intimidated by all of the bigger guys—and they were *all* bigger. My body had betrayed me. One incident was particularly humiliating. It was very early in our freshman year, and we had just finished our PE class. Everyone had to take showers. Everyone. I did my best to get out of it, but I simply wasn't allowed. I had to take a shower, and ended up choosing the lesser of two humiliations. After all of the guys had finished, I stripped down to my underwear, stepped into the shower in my underwear, and turned the shower on. I stood under the water for the longest thirty seconds of my life and quickly got out of the shower. I cannot remember if the other boys were there or not. That was one of many humiliations that year that gave me a rude awakening to the new world in which I was living—high school—where the Rules went to the next level. It was very clear to me that I no longer fit in; I was no longer cool. And I definitely was still just a boy in a world where developing into a man was the most important rite of passage.

I would stare at my naked body over and over again in the mirror, cursing myself and God. I wouldn't shower for days. I started having night terrors. I'd sleep over at a friend's house and have the night terrors there as well. I almost punched a friend's grandfather when he came to check on me because I had been screaming and cursing in my sleep. I refused to stay the night at friends' houses after that. I became genuinely afraid for my sanity, yet somehow was still able to attend school day after day. Was it any wonder I was such a huge discipline problem?

My sophomore year was full of more suffering: crying myself to sleep almost every night, praying to God that I would just grow, and suffering my father's rage and abuse when he wasn't passed out in various rooms throughout the house. I had such deep shame that I spoke to nobody. I even desperately tried to make my voice change simply by talking deeper. I did everything I could to give some semblance of having hit puberty. It was daily torture. If I had already been hypervigilant from growing up in an alcoholic home, I was now *hyper*-hypervigilant. I was traumatized.

Finally, after some help from a guidance counselor, Brother Paul, and my father walking into my room after I carved "Fuck You" into my arm, I was taken to our family doctor who referred me to a specialist at Georgetown University Hospital. I was medically treated with shots of testosterone for six months over the summer between my sophomore and junior years of high school. During this time, nobody—absolutely nobody—offered me any kind of compassion or empathy. They either said nothing or made what I now realize were very insensitive and inappropriate jokes and comments. Nobody told me that this didn't make me defective, that it wasn't my fault, or that there was nothing wrong with me. I had already spent two years coming to the conclusion that I was broken and being punished by "God," and this was never challenged by anyone in my family or anyone at school. Adding emotional injury to insult, my father was too drunk to drive me to get one of the last shots, so I drove myself. Here I was at sixteen, hoping desperately to shed the boy-skin in which I was stuck, driving myself to the final appointment to receive the "magic serum" medically pushing me into manhood.

Early in my recovery I met some men, including my first sponsor, who had had similar experiences, but these did not seem to have been nearly as traumatic for them as for me. They also did not grow up in a violent home. Or maybe it was the difference in our personalities. But my reaction to everything that happened between ages fourteen and sixteen was extreme and profound. My intelligence, voracious introspection, and pathological sensitivity all worked against me, making everything worse. I obsessed about it daily and knew that every boy, girl, man, and woman was looking at me and "knew." They knew I was just a boy. They were laughing at me. God was doing this to me. It became a deeply existential crisis. I was convinced that I was not a "real" young man. I was broken, ugly, and weak, and felt like a freak.

Now, when I tell this part of my story in my trainings and workshops, other men begin to open up about similar experiences—men like me, who you would not think were walking around ten, twenty, even thirty years later still feeling like a little powerless, scrawny kid. A truth I have discovered is that many men can identify with this type of experience to varying degrees. This is a trauma many of us have been carrying around, hidden deep inside us, for far too long.

I recently met with a young guy who looked *exactly* like me when I was eighteen: dark hair, short, tan, with a slender build. It was emotional as I looked into this mirror. I asked him as gently as I could how old he was. "Eighteen." My heart sank for him as I projected my pain onto him and empathized with his situation. I shared a little bit about my experience and saw the sadness enter his face. I mentioned being medically treated to grow, and another young man in the same treatment program told me about his struggle with being small and not hitting puberty until his junior year and what that was like for him. Finally, there was another young man who also said that he had been scrawny long into his high school years and that he still struggled with those self-images. In his case it led to an unhealthy obsession with weight lifting and bodybuilding.

The truth is that as a prepubescent young man I stood *outside* the usual images of masculinity. I started to see the Water, not because I consciously and thoughtfully reflected on the Man Rules, but because I *was not* a man. As I felt myself in the Water, I also felt the dissonance between what seemed to be the ideal masculinity and *me*. I was drowning in the Water and desperate to find some degree of solace. Burning in my psyche was this constant and resounding voice telling me that I was not a man. I believed it. That voice haunted me. The worst part was that once I grew to almost six feet tall and matured into what many people consider to be a handsome man, it was too late. The damage had been done. Like anorexics wasting away on death's door who still see themselves as fat, it has taken twenty-plus years for me to not see the gaunt, prepubescent five-foot boy looking back at me in the mirror. And he can still show up when I'm under stress or feeling threatened.

From my sophomore year of high school until my senior year of college, one thing helped to quiet the voices and allowed me to feel less insane and a little more comfortable around people: alcohol and other drugs. In that sense, initially, they saved my life. I needed numbness. And, of course, that boomeranged very quickly. When you search for sanity by turning to something that is known to destroy sanity, your problems are likely to get worse. The relief didn't last long and I spiraled out of control, still tortured by the voice telling me I was not a man, that I was a freak.

Alcohol and pot served another important purpose, though: They were the only tools I had to help me talk to girls. Before I hit puberty I could talk to girls, but even in my most drunken state I had to be hypervigilant so that I didn't get too close or have my shameful secret found out. One girl in particular thought I was funny and cute and I started talking to her on the phone after New Year's Eve of my sophomore year, and then I realized, why am I talking to her? There was no way I could go on a date with her. Or be intimate with her in any way. So I just stopped calling her. That was what helped put me over the edge and led to the cutting incident that brought me to the attention of medical professionals.

Even when I finally hit puberty, I continued to look for evidence that I was still not a man. I didn't have enough hair under my arms and none on my chest, I had no real muscle tone, and I hadn't yet started to shave. I started drinking more and smoking pot, which made it easier for me to meet more young women. They liked me. They thought I was cute and funny. They liked that I was smart and self-deprecating. But I still didn't date. I went on *one* date in high school. It was with a young woman who one summer worked at the same telemarketing business as me, and I only asked her out because my friend, a quintessential stud visiting from Australia, asked her sister out. I had no idea how to talk to her or be with her, and yet somehow I was still able to lose my virginity to her. And that was also humiliating. I did not have a clue what I was doing or that it was extremely common for young men to experience orgasm within seconds of penetration. I only saw it as more evidence that I was not a man and that there was something wrong with my body.

When I started working out to build muscle, my only coach was the voice inside my head constantly calling me a "pussy," a "wimp," and every epithet a young man can hurl at himself to bench-press a little more weight or do a few more curls. No matter how much muscle I may have developed, I still could only see myself as a puny weakling. My wife would often comment on my muscular body or how I compared to other guys at the beach, and my first thought was (1) *She is making fun of me,* or (2) *She is lying to me.* It has taken a long time for me to see my body accurately, as it is rather than as it was. When I was forty years old and writing this book, Nancy encouraged me to walk down the airport walkways and notice how many men I was actually taller than. I laughed it off when she suggested it, but when I did it I was amazed that I was taller than 80 to 85 percent of the men I encountered.

Under the influence or not, the shame I felt about my body and about not being a man was constant and had me always on guard. The saying that "addicts don't get into relationships, they take hostages" was absolutely true for me. I lured women in as a nice guy, but if they got too close to me or hit any of my wounds, I reacted intensely. I became my father. I was an asshole. Mean. Enraged. Abusive. I watched a person whom I barely recognized come out of me. And that just added more fuel to the fire of shame that burned inside me.

My life changed irrevocably in 1994, my senior year of college, in two very important ways. I discovered the concept of gender, and I was confronted by multiple people about my use of alcohol and other drugs, and consequently got into recovery. Those two forces coming together offered me more hope than I had ever felt in my entire life. I learned that gender-based reality was painful for a lot of people. As a result of the social upheaval of the late 1960s and early 1970s, there were people thinking very actively and critically about the expectations around how women and men "perform" our scripts for gender. Because of my experience in adolescence I was more than eager to listen to those who were deconstructing male expectations. My process of recovery gave me permission to begin to give voice to the incredibly painful emotions and thoughts that were killing me from the inside out. I also learned something even more powerful from both of these experiences: *I was not alone*. I began to see the Water more clearly.

But the shame ran deep, and recovery made it harder to hide all of the pain. I started to learn how to talk to people sober. I learned how to just hang out and have friends. I learned how to connect. I wanted to connect with others so badly. That was always a core part of who I was, and still am. Slowly but surely, I began to learn how to crawl socially, then walk, and then even run. It was terrifying at times. Other times it felt like I was destined to be alone for the rest of my life. Long into my recovery I carried the shame and the feelings of worthlessness from my trauma around with me. It controlled so much of my life, yet I was still unable to talk about it.

Every relationship I ever had was affected by the core belief that there was something wrong with me, and that I was not a man. When I was still active in my addiction, I would only have one-night stands with women. That continued in recovery, despite it being generally against my values. I rarely connected with women in other ways, not because I was trying to be mean or hurtful, but because I was scared shitless. I didn't have a relationship longer than a month until I was twenty-two years old, and that was long-distance. After that, no relationship lasted longer than a month until I was twenty-five, when the woman I was seeing actually asked me if I was interested in her or just trying to stay in a relationship longer than a month! I was unable to let anyone get too close. The women usually ended up breaking up with me long before I broke up with them. Any woman with the slightest amount of self-esteem would drop me as soon as she got a glimpse of my darker side. Sadly, part of the Woman Rules is that women are supposed to put up with that guy and be able to change him. Several tried with me, but not for long.

I would not be naked in front of women. I would never raise my arms. I spent every second I had with any girlfriend wondering how she could be interested in me. I could never trust that she would stay with me. Or really like me. Or want to be with me over someone else—someone manlier. If I was drunk, that didn't matter as much. However, once the special elixir wore off, I was left to face me, and one look in the mirror was all I needed to be reminded that any woman who was with me was a fool. And a liar. And just waiting to find someone better.

That was my experience for a very long time, even in recovery. It made it easy for me to choose the work I did for my master's degree, as well as the focus I have now. At some deeply emotional level it has all been about trying to prove to myself and the world that I am a man. As silly as it may sound, it is true.

This is only a small part of my story but a huge part of the trauma that has shaped my perceptions of myself as man, as well as the man I have become. I now spend a lot of my time going around the country talking with others about the Man Rules and their effects upon how men see and conduct themselves. It is amazing to me, despite how much personal work I have done, how often the Rules control my behavior and lead me to act in ways that are contrary to the man I truly aspire to be. I write this not in a spirit of self-shaming, but rather to impress upon you just how tenacious these Rules are. You may very much want to be a different man than you are, but you also find that you are controlled by the Rules more than you ever realized. And until you can see the Water you swim in, you don't even know these Rules exist.

We all have our own stories about how we have become the men we are now. Chances are there are aspects of your experience that worked for you and that align with the man you want to be. There are also probably aspects of your experience that do not align with the man you want to be. All of these experiences combine to become *your* story of becoming a man.

I have discovered something very important ever since I found the courage to bring my inquiry about masculinity out into the world, and my guess is that this also applies to you: *Every man* I have spoken with or heard from has some kind of conversation happening inside him, questioning how much of a man he is. Very few men feel completely secure and grounded in their masculinity. When they are being truly honest, very few can say they feel deeply confident in their masculinity and their sense of being a *real man*. Of course, that is the problem with so much of this: What is a real man? Is being a real man solely defined by society? Of course not. Ultimately, it is different for each of us, but it is essential that we reflect on our ideas about what it means to be a man, and the degree to which we have blindly followed the Rules.

Today, as I stated above, I have been happily married for ten years, with a beautiful four-year-old daughter. I am fairly confident in who I am and basically comfortable in my skin. You would never look at me and have any idea about what I have been through or the road I have traveled to become the man I am today. What is most important about that statement is that you can say the exact same thing about every man—you have no idea what his journey has been to become the man you now see. That is why our stories are so important and why I have shared mine. It is in telling our stories that we get to reinforce who we are and create the man we want to be. As sharing our stories transforms us, our map and everything charted upon it is also transformed. We have the opportunity to own our stories—or they will continue to own us.

Into Action

In your notebook, set aside about ten blank pages. Begin to write your story. Focus on specific intervals of your life based on age (0–5, 6–10, 11–15, 16–20, 21–25, etc.) or specific milestones (childhood, grade school, middle school, high school, etc.) until you get to your present age. Allow each interval to have at least its own page, front and back. For each interval, write your story of becoming a boy or a man during that time, as applicable. Answer the following questions for each interval:

- ► What ways of behaving were considered acceptable?
- ► What ways of behaving were considered unacceptable?
- ► How did boys/men treat you?
- ► How did girls/women treat you?
- ► What are some of the more difficult memories you have from this period of your life as related to your becoming a boy or a man?
- ► What are some of the best memories you have from this period of your life as related to your becoming a boy or a man?
- ► What were some of the biggest Man Rules operating in your life at that time?

Share some or all of your story with your partner, sponsor, and/or a trusted friend.

CHAPTER THREE
Men, Relationships, and Trauma

"Through recovery I reshaped my beliefs of what being a man really is. Subsequently, I look at trauma as something that I don't have to duck and hide from, and with the help of others, I move through it in an authentic manner." —Mike

"My first sexual experience was with my adopted sister. She was sixteen, I was seven." —Roland

"Forty-eight years of emotional abuse by a society that doesn't accept men who have sex with men. Forty-eight years as an African-American walking on eggshells at times." —David

"The shame of severe poverty, being referred to as a half-breed in a full-blood world, and the boarding school drove me to alcohol and other drugs and nearly destroyed me." —Rod

The concept of trauma is absolutely essential to understanding the terrain over which we are traveling. Have you ever found yourself on a road trip or going for a walk and you encounter various obstacles that were not on the map you were using to guide you? You may not even be sure what the obstacles are or how to overcome them. You just know you are stuck.

Most of the men I've talked to over the years who are on the journey of recovery can identify some point in their lives when they realized it was not okay to express certain feelings and discuss particular behaviors or recount certain experiences, especially if these showed weakness, vulnerability, or sensitivity. Crying, above all, was strictly discouraged. These restrictions were not made up in our heads. They came from the Man Rules and what these Rules tell us.

We learned, sometimes through everyday interactions with other men but frequently because of abuse or other traumatic experiences, that the only appropriate way to express feelings like fear, hurt, rejection, or sadness was through the conduit of anger and violence. For the longest time I thought that meant that all men were like me, full of rage and bad tempered; but that is not the case at all. Anger happens along a continuum. Some men stuff their anger and it comes out through isolation and cold silence, and can lead to severe depression. In fact, I wasn't always full of rage or temperamental; far from it. The point is that we have all of these emotions, and for many of us they get "stuffed" and held inside us and come out as some form of anger.

One of the most powerful breakthroughs in addiction recovery is our growing understanding of trauma. My friend, Jamie Marich, PhD, has a wonderful analogy she uses in her work to make trauma easier to understand. She reminds us that the word *trauma* is Greek for "wound." She talks about all of the different kinds of wounds that exist—open wounds (lacerations, abrasions, punctures) vs. closed wounds (contusions, hematomas, crush injuries, or slowly developing chronic wounds)—and the different ways those wounds heal. As she describes, "For some people, simple traumas (wounds) can clear up on their own, but for others with more complicating emotional variables (many of which can be biologically based), the healing process may take longer. If an individual who has experienced a major emotional trauma doesn't obtain the proper conditions to heal (which can include formal mental health treatment), it will likely take longer for the trauma to clear up, and it could end up causing other symptoms. Of course, the wound is never going to get better; in all likelihood, it will worsen." And just like a physical wound, when someone experiences a traumatic event, he or she becomes susceptible to "rewounding" or being retraumatized. When other people in his or her life (sometimes including helping professionals) keep unintentionally disturbing the wound through words or actions that tap into the trauma, healing never takes place.

Mental health practitioners now understand that one of the distinguishing factors with trauma is not the event itself as much as an individual's response to the event. How people respond to events varies widely, and that response is influenced by numerous factors, including how the environment responds, especially one's family and community. What was traumatic for me might not be for you. Even people from the same family can have dramatically different responses to the same event. Especially as children, we should not be expected to have to deal with traumatic experiences on our own. Children should be able to depend on a safe and supportive home environment. Sadly, that is often not the case. It does not have to be a violent home for a young boy to get the clear message that expressing his pain and sharing his pain with others is unwelcome, and even unsafe. For a lot of us, that was part of the training we got from our parents and community, and it is a form of rewounding.

Another important concept related to trauma is what Francine Shapiro, PhD, the developer of Eye Movement Desensitization and Reprocessing (EMDR), a research-based trauma treatment, refers to as "big-T" and "small-t" traumas. Don't be confused; "small" doesn't mean the trauma is any less significant. It means it is easier to miss because it happens over an extended period of time and is often not seen or even treated as trauma. Big-T traumas are the ones that have a clear beginning and end. You can identify details regarding where you were, what you were doing, what happened to you, and what was happening around you. Big-T traumas can be car accidents, natural disasters, experiences in war, attacks or assaults, and so on. They tend to have a life-threatening dimension to them. The idea is that the individual is relatively stable and grounded in his or her life, and this experience is jarring and significantly impacts the individual's sense of physical and/or emotional safety.

Small-t traumas are very common for people in recovery, especially for those of us who grew up in addicted and chaotic family systems. The example I give in trainings is having an abusive alcoholic father and trying to figure out the details around specific incidents. Was he drunk? Was it daytime or nighttime? Was he getting angry at the same thing he had laughed at a week earlier? Was he passed out, or was he wreaking havoc? Was it Tuesday or Thursday or Saturday? Was it when I was six, twelve, or twenty? There are so many more subtle details, and they can be so different depending on certain circumstances that it is difficult to narrow them down. There are many examples of small-t trauma: the kid who is bullied for being overweight or is treated as an outcast because he comes from a poor family or neighborhood or is effeminate or is of a different race.

The cumulative impacts of these small-t traumas can remain hidden from the affected individual. He tells himself they do not matter or are not important or are simply "the way things are." They become "normal." He tells himself, and perhaps others tell him, that he should just get over them, so he tries to not think about them and suppresses the feelings associated with them. The thoughts and feelings are still there, but they have not been emotionally processed. When this boy grows up, and as an adult gets into a primary relationship that even remotely brings up memories of such past experiences, these small-t traumas can be triggered—without him or his partner having any knowledge of what is happening. On the surface it seems that there is a major emotional reaction completely out of proportion to an argument or some situation, when in fact a past trauma has been triggered.

And this can easily happen inadvertently. An example from my life is when I would walk around naked in front of Nancy. If she saw my body and didn't have a positive reaction, I took her lack of response to be a lack of attraction, or even disgust. I did not know that I was reacting like that, but it would often lead to a fight or my putting her down or being rejecting toward her because I had a deep wound of shame that had been incidentally triggered. That is the key: Previous traumas will be triggered unknowingly in your most intimate relationships. If you are unaware of this phenomenon and/or not paying attention to how it can play out in your relationship, you and the person you're in a relationship with will end up upset, as well as confused as to what is the *real* issue. This happens to men all the time, because if they are not emotionally aware of what is happening and do not catch the feelings at an early stage, then they get carried away on a wave of anger that may have little to do with what is occurring in the present. And when the explosion of anger takes place, many of us make it the other person's fault. They unwittingly touch our wound, and we get pissed off at them.

The truth is that a lot of men dismiss small-t traumas as something they should "just get over." In some cases we've heard it, and may even continue to hear it from our loved ones and, for those of us in twelve-step recovery, our peers and sponsors. A common message in recovery is "You just need to work the steps harder." Know this: However small it (the traumatic issue) may seem, it *is* important. It *does* matter. It is *not* just a small thing. And struggling with it *does not* make you less of a man. The steps may very well be part of the solution, but that doesn't mean they are the sole solution.

What is important for you to understand is that if the issue causes you discomfort, then it is real. If it is something you have been struggling with for some time, it is not likely that you will be able to simply "get over it"; otherwise you would have done so by now. Sadly, the voices telling us we are not working hard enough in our recovery or that we are doing something wrong only reinforce the shame we feel about whatever is causing us such distress. The real healing starts by talking about it, and that means having people in your life whom you trust, people you know will not laugh at you or judge you no matter how foolish, weak, or ashamed you feel about the issue. Mike said, "I have found it important to put some time and distance between me and the traumatic event. To back away, breathe, and just feel. Then I need to connect with one of my go-to guys and hear myself talk about the experience, to gain perspective, and to feel safe. After that I'm in a better position to deal with whatever is necessary." That is an excellent approach to follow whenever issues connected to past trauma come up and cause you discomfort and distress.

I started sponsoring a man named Joe who had seven years in recovery. He knew my passion for helping men move into an area of what we call "emotional recovery." I ask the hard questions and create as safe a space as I can for the man to talk. And I listen. I hear him. And I am not restricted by the Twelve Steps or the philosophy and literature of the various fellowships. As much as I love that part of recovery, I also firmly believe in seeking "outside help," as advocated in the book *Alcoholics Anonymous*: "God has abundantly supplied this world with fine doctors, psychologists, and practitioners of various kinds. Do not hesitate to take your health problems to such persons." This fact is often overlooked by some twelve-step fundamentalists.

Joe mentioned to me that he hadn't slept in his own bed, or even in his own house, for almost two years. He was spending a lot of time sleeping at the homes of friends. He came up with good excuses for doing this. What really impressed me was that he had some close friends whom he felt safe enough to open up to and they, in return, had opened their homes to him. I did not suggest that he work a step about his lack of faith or do a fear inventory from the Fourth Step, or suggest that this was due to some defect of character. Grown men with seven years of recovery don't fear sleeping in their bed because there is something wrong with their recovery. They do it because of trauma.

Joe started seeing an experienced trauma therapist specializing in EMDR. He began to see that his difficulties started after his parents divorced (again) and worsened after he broke up with a girlfriend. Importantly, rather than engaging in an extensive regimen of talk therapy sessions, Joe learned a technique known as Emotional Freedom Technique (EFT). EFT is a process of tapping on key acupressure points, breathing, and doing positive repetitive self-talk. Joe began to see how shame and anxiety from these past experiences affected his ability to sleep peacefully in his bed. He also started slowly challenging himself to do things differently. But equally important, through EMDR and EFT Joe was able to rewire his brain and adjust the faulty connections created as a result of small-t traumas he experienced as a child that had been triggered in adulthood.

The brain plays a central role in the processing of traumatic experiences. Trauma has a profound impact on our brain and our body. The triune brain—a model proposed by the American physician and neuroscientist Paul D. MacLean and endorsed widely by trauma experts—includes the primitive or reptilian part of our brain, the limbic system, and the neocortex. When it comes to understanding and healing from trauma, the limbic system and the neocortex are critical. From an evolutionary perspective, the reptilian part of our brain is the oldest and most basic part of our brain. It is the part that we have in common with many animals and controls our most basic functions. The limbic system is the seat of all of our emotions and is also where the "fight-or-flight" response lives. The neocortex is the command center of the brain and what separates us from all other animals. The neocortex is what gives humans the abilities for abstract thinking, moral reasoning, delay of gratification, speech, and the capacity to process past experiences to use what we have learned to inform our decisions in the present.

The relationship between the limbic system and the neocortex has profound importance. As Jamie Marich explains, "for a person with unprocessed trauma symptoms, the three regions of the brain are not optimally communicating with each other. Indeed, during periods of intense emotional disturbance, a human being cannot optimally access the functions of the neocortex because the limbic, or emotional brain, is in control." The limbic system is activated during traumatic experiences to help the person survive via fight, flight, or freeze. Resolving trauma involves creating new neural pathways reestablishing the linkage between the limbic system and the neocortex. Only then does a person regain the ability to process traumatic events, make sense of them and the emotions with which they are connected, and place them in the appropriate context where they can be understood and integrated into the person's overall experience.

I lived in my limbic system for most of my recovery. The slightest event would trigger an emotional reaction, and BAM! I was in fight-or-flight mode—mostly fight, because again, as men we are trained to ignore the fear, and fight. Moreover, flight or running away is unmanly and violates the Rules. This neural connection was built and then reinforced over years and even decades of emotional instability and repeated triggering/activation. Over and over again many misperceived cues and triggers had me jumping right into my limbic system, and then I was being driven by my emotions and my shame—a toxic combination.

There are a lot of people in the rooms of recovery with untreated trauma, some of which even rises to the level of post-traumatic stress disorder (PTSD). The problem for decades, particularly for men, has been our tendency to focus on the diagnosis of PTSD, which is on the far end of the continuum of trauma. As a result, we have missed a lot of male trauma. Trauma occurs when, after a traumatic experience (or experiences), people become and remain stuck operating out of their limbic system. The impact on one's life becomes significant enough that it has serious impact on our ability to engage in everyday activities and live a productive life.

As Lily Burana, a woman who has written with courage, humor, and vulnerability about her experiences, describes it, "The overload of stress makes your panic button touchier than most people's, so certain things trigger a stress reaction—or more candidly—an overreaction. Sometimes, the panic button gets stuck altogether and you're in a state of constant alert, buzzing and twitchy and aggressive. You can tell yourself, 'it's okay,' but your wily brain is already ten steps ahead of the game, registering danger and sounding the alarm. The long-range result is that the peace of mind you deserve in the present is held hostage by the terror of your past."

Can't you just hear the pain in that description? Can you feel it in your body? What does trauma *feel* like to you? Not just in your brain, but what does it feel like in your body? Can you notice the physical cues when you are getting ready to go "off-line"? Literally, that is what is happening. It may feel like a super-quick shutdown, but there is a complex process happening, and the more you can learn to notice it, know what your triggers are, be in your body, do conscious breathing, and use other tools, the more you can slow the process down and even interrupt it.

Here's a specific example of this for me: For the first seventeen years of my recovery I used to be on the verge of panic attacks when I went into any public restroom by myself. Did you catch that? I said seventeen years—not seventeen months or even seven years. The door would shut and I feared for my safety. Every time the door opened I had this feeling I was going to be attacked. I imagined it and felt it. For the longest time

I never talked about this because I was embarrassed. Essentially, I told myself to "man up" and suffered with that panic for years. It didn't make sense, because I was a grown man merely going to the bathroom. It got better, so I figured that was good enough. But it never went away. I didn't know it was a symptom of trauma. I finally brought it up when I started seeing a trauma therapist and made a commitment to tell him *everything*. It was the most honest I had ever been with anyone in my life. That was in 2012, when I was long into my recovery and even my trauma recovery. The Rules have a very powerful way of keeping us silent. It isn't until you start to truly breathe again that you realize how much you had been suffocating.

Now some in the recovery community might say the problem is that I didn't work a thorough Fourth Step. It's just a fear, Dan. You had all of the tools you needed with the Twelve Steps. You didn't need to go to a professional. Or maybe they'll say that I needed to look more honestly at Steps Six and Seven because it is a defect of character showing itself. Or I just had to pray every time I went into a bathroom. And after. And whenever I thought about going to the bathroom. Unfortunately, sometimes in recovery we shame people into trying to work a better recovery program. I used to be guilty of it myself, assuming that the standard tools of recovery would be sufficient to overcome all pain and tragedy.

Shaming behaviors contradict the spirit of recovery. However, that doesn't mean there isn't some truth to those step-related comments. There is absolutely no question that the steps and other tools of twelve-step recovery can help men better deal with their most painful experiences. Almost every man I interviewed talked about how the steps, particularly Steps Four and Five and Eight and Nine, have helped them significantly in sorting through the pain of their past. There is no question there is something powerful about the power of prayer; it transforms our thinking and, in brain parlance, helps to create new neural connections.

The bottom line is that it's important to understand that if you've had a traumatic experience and still suffer from it, this does not mean you're weak, sick, or in any way at fault. More often than not, that's just the Rules talking. The Rules are co-conspirators with trauma. They hide trauma. Our desperate attempts to be men often keep us from seeing our trauma and/or how much it has affected us. Only a few of the men I interviewed identified no trauma in their lives.

As Peter A. Levine, PhD, one of the leading authorities on understanding trauma, says in his book, *Healing Trauma*, "Recently, *trauma* has been used as a buzzword to replace everyday stress, as in, 'I had a traumatic day at work.' However, this use is completely misleading. While it is true that all traumatic events are stressful, all stressful events are not traumatic." This notwithstanding, he goes on to say ". . . almost all of us have experienced some form of trauma, either directly or indirectly." Put simply, per Bessel van der Kolk, MD, also among the world's foremost experts, trauma occurs when an external threat overwhelms an individual's internal and external *positive* coping mechanisms. So, if your first reaction is to say that you don't have trauma, it may well be a defensive reaction—a way of proclaiming or even protecting your masculinity.

Until you have quietly reflected on this issue and looked into it at some length with an open mind, you may not know whether or not you have experienced any trauma. What I can say is that I know far too many men who have lived with trauma for many years of their recovery with no awareness that trauma was at the root of their suffering and feelings of disconnection. Do not let contempt prior to investigation prevent you from exploring something that could offer you a degree of peace and freedom you never thought possible.

The challenge a lot of men have is that they do not necessarily see their experiences as traumatic because they compare them to other people's traumas—what they might consider "real" or more serious trauma, consistent with the big-T-versus-small-t trauma distinction. Many men probably look at their small-t traumatic experiences in hindsight with an adult's understanding, saying to themselves something to the effect of "I see how this could be traumatic for a six-year-old, but I am forty years old now and it's not a big deal. I am over it. That was a long time ago." That is the danger. Our brain, particularly our brain's limbic system, does not care about our age, then or now. And it maintains the emotional memories of those experiences, no matter how long ago they occurred. That is why people's trauma reactions can be triggered so long after the original events took place. Our bodies also carry the memories of traumatic events, and we may have physiological reactions to external stimuli without realizing that this is a common trauma response.

Even long into doing the work on my own trauma, it took me some time before it became clear that my experiences related to delayed growth and physical maturation, along with the violence at home and misery at high school, were significant traumas for me that had far-reaching effects on my life. For the longest time I had minimized it despite the incredible body dysmorphia and horribly negative internal scripts that defined my sense of being a man. I am still making peace with the deep trauma I experienced as a result of not growing.

Often our desperate attempts to be strong and powerful as men end up hurting people, especially ourselves. Frequently this happens as collateral damage of the trauma-based war waged inside us. The less we see and understand our trauma, the more damage it causes. When trauma remains unacknowledged and untreated, men in recovery—even long-term recovery—may find themselves alienated from others, including their twelve-step communities, and abusing loved ones, destroying their marriages, struggling with relapse, and acting out in other ways that damage themselves and others. As Luke said, "Without having the tools to deal with my trauma in a healthy way, I either avoided it or wallowed in it and blamed others."

A man can work the steps rigorously, but the emotional, physical, and psychological fallout of untreated trauma will keep him stuck in the pain, confusion, depression, anger, and hopelessness of addictive and other unhealthy behaviors. Those around him might see him as a "dry drunk" even though he has been in recovery for years. The vast majority of the men who continue to act like "tornadoes in the lives of others" do not want to be that guy. But they act in ways that make it hard, often really hard, to have compassion for them. We have to help men find ways to see the harm they cause when acting out on their trauma while fostering compassion for them so they can become compassionate toward themselves.

The first steps toward healing happen when we give ourselves permission to acknowledge the emotional impact of our experiences.

This is critical, because men who stay abstinent for a year or more without beginning to address their trauma are the *exception,* not the rule. There is no question in my mind that the number-one factor in relapse for people recently out of treatment, during their first years in recovery, and even in later years, is undiagnosed and untreated trauma. It's not because they didn't go to enough meetings or because they didn't work the steps well enough. While that may be part of the picture, it is rarely the only reason. If someone is telling you that, then chances are they have little awareness of trauma, including possibly their own.

Untreated trauma is insidious. There is probably nothing that is more destructive to our relationships. Again, because of the Rules, we tend not to see trauma. If you have struggled with relapse or have found yourself struggling with other forms of addiction in your recovery, and nobody has ever talked to you about or assessed you for trauma, this is an area that may be important for you to explore. Find a professional who knows what he or she is talking about and get the support and services that can help you.

Men's Trauma

My recovery was severely limited as I attempted to heal through the painful effects of trauma without knowing that's what I was struggling with. Among the effects of my trauma was that my relationships were also severely limited. The idea common in the twelve-step community of being "happy, joyous, and free" felt elusive to me.

In the years I have been working with men in recovery I've come to realize how prevalent hidden trauma is. As essential as it is to recognize trauma and its effects, we also need to understand the reality of men's gender-specific experience of trauma. How men experience, respond to, express the symptoms of, and heal from trauma is often (though not always) different from women. And that's primarily because of those damn Man Rules. "The Eight Points of Agreement Regarding Males, Trauma, and Addiction," (see Appendix A) is a document created when, with funding from a private family foundation, I was able to bring a group of national experts together to focus greater attention on the issue of male trauma. I had the privilege of visualizing and organizing the summit out of which this document came. To date it is one of the most significant professional experiences I have had. This is part of the map to help you in your recovery.

"Asshole"

As I like to say in the trainings I do, "What is a word we commonly use for a man who has trauma? Asshole." Isn't that interesting? Have you ever thought that when you act like an asshole it could be because you have had some kind of trauma triggered and you do not know how to deal with the pain of it so you act in ways that push people away? You react before you even know what you are doing. Does that sound at all familiar? Have you ever thought that about the other men in your life when they are acting that way? Maybe you are in a relationship— romantic, professional, or friend—with a man who acts like an asshole. Have you ever thought that it could be trauma? Can you cultivate the compassion necessary to support him while making it clear that mean or abusive behavior is unacceptable?

The feeling of being "Jekyll and Hyde" haunted me during those first twelve years in recovery, and I never understood it. I thought those kinds of wild emotional swings were supposed to be over once I got through early recovery. I had a secret I kept from the people closest to me in my community and even from myself. The shame was debilitating. I didn't talk about it in meetings. In fact, I was deeply invested in looking good in my twelve-step meetings because I had five years in recovery. Then ten years. Yet, all the while I was slowly dying inside and becoming more and more afraid that I would never be able to feel close to anyone without feeling like it was ripping me apart.

Of course, men are rarely encouraged to talk about their experiences of abuse or trauma, and our culture seems very confused about what is acceptable behavior both from and toward boys and men. The historical silence surrounding the issue of the sexual abuse of boys began to break with the Catholic clergy sex abuse scandal. The sex abuse scandal at Penn State University reinforced that sexual abuse, one of the types of trauma that has the most ignorance and stigma associated with it, even happens to the young men we view as the toughest and the best representatives of masculinity. There have been some other notable events that have helped to erode our societal denial regarding the sexual abuse of men. In October of 2010 Tyler Perry talked about his own sexual abuse, and in November of 2010 Oprah Winfrey aired an episode focusing on men's experience of sexual abuse. Two hundred men came forward about sexual abuse they had experienced. Even more powerful, their loved ones heard these stories—many for the first time—and were then interviewed for the next show.

We have started to make an increasingly clear connection between the violence and abuse perpetrated on boys and men, how men are raised in this society, and the violence men commit. Every man I spoke with during the writing of this book had experienced some kind of emotional or verbal abuse, and many talked about physical abuse as well. Some of their stories are heartbreaking. They run the gamut of abuse, from extreme verbal and emotional abuse to racism, to sexual abuse by both men and women, to the systematic abuse perpetrated at the boarding schools that Native Americans were forced to endure in the late nineteenth and early twentieth centuries. The silence that many men feel forced to keep around these traumatic experiences of abuse causes a great deal of pain and, not surprisingly, often becomes a factor in their addictive behaviors down the line. That was also the experience of the men I interviewed for *A Man's Way through the Twelve Steps*.

Knowing that abuse and violence against boys and men and the resulting trauma are so strongly linked with addiction, and knowing that if they are left untreated the aftermath of these experiences can cause undeniable psychological, relational, physical, and spiritual destruction, it seems not only logical but also mandatory that we should offer help and healing opportunities not just for the addictive behavior on the surface, but for the trauma-based pain and fears that underlie and feed it.

The challenge for men is in being able to overcome years of socialization and, in effect, training that have reinforced separateness, isolation, emotional illiteracy, and varying degrees of relational incompetence. Bobby said, "I have had to challenge my internalized ideas of masculinity around strength and self-reliance in order to examine a self-defeating pattern of automatic responses that did not serve me or others in seeking healthy outcomes." When men get into intimate relationships and find their partners wanting, even begging for, communication, vulnerability, and openness, they often freeze up or are deeply scared by that level of intimacy.

Although men and women may come at relationships from different perspectives, they both want and need relationships and desire connection, authenticity, emotional openness, and vulnerability. One of the primary purposes of this book is to support men in looking at all of the barriers that keep them from cocreating and engaging in healthy relationships. These barriers are more than just trauma, but there is no question that trauma plays a central role. Importantly, as Ray pointed out, some of our ideas about being men actually help us: "They [these ideas about being a man] have given me the courage and the desire to go through the healing process." Remember, the Man Rules have some positive aspects.

What is the likelihood that *you* have trauma? My guess is very high. The following are some questions related to signs of trauma. On a separate piece of paper, answer each question with a number one through five, based on the following scale:

0 = Never   1 = Rarely   2 = Sometimes   3 = Often   4 = Very Often   5 = Always

- How often do you yell at other people or put them down in hurtful ways?

- How often do you find yourself mistreating your partner and sometimes feeling as though you are "possessed" or are two different people?

- When you feel close to someone, how often do you find yourself shutting down or becoming full of rage toward her or him?

- How often do you mock your partner or become uncomfortable when he or she cries or expresses vulnerability?

- When you feel sad or hurt, how often do you turn to anger or isolate in depression?

- How often do you overreact to conflict with extreme engagement or avoidance?

- How easily startled are you?

- How often do you find yourself struggling with violent reactions, thoughts, and fantasies on a regular basis?

- How often do you push others away with sarcasm, ridicule, or abuse when they are getting too close?

- How often do you push away people you love and care about, using anger to protect yourself from being hurt?

- How often do you have visions or fantasies of hurting those you love?

Do any of these sound familiar? If so, it is information, not a scientific assessment or diagnosis. However, it probably merits a conversation with a professional who understands trauma. You are not crazy. You are not a bad person. But you may need help to heal. Give yourself and your loved ones that gift.

As we continue the discussion of relationships throughout this book, I would ask you to keep this information in mind. I invite you to come back to this chapter over and over. Let it wash over you and sink in. I realize that some of you reading this do not have trauma; however, I have known far too many men who have been lost in the pain of trauma and had no idea. At some level they had told themselves they did not have trauma. That's all you have to do. Tell yourself you do not have trauma, and it becomes true in your thinking. Keep in mind that the Rules have an influential role in convincing men they don't have trauma:

"It's not a big deal."

"Don't be such a pussy, it wasn't that bad." (Notice the antifemale nuance to this one.)

"You're weak if you admit that you were abused."

"Get over it."

"You deserved it."

These and numerous other messages make up a cold chorus of self-hate and toxic shame. Mike talked about it this way: "Unfortunately, I believe the shame carried by a lot of men prevents them from recognizing, acknowledging, and dealing with trauma. I grew up hearing the message 'If I see you crying, I'll give you something to cry about.' With those beliefs ingrained in many of us, it's tough to deal effectively with trauma."

Relationships with Trauma

For many men, whenever they are encouraged to attempt greater intimacy in their closest relationships, they are being invited back into traumatic experiences from their childhood. What are the characteristics of a healthy relationship? They include intimacy, trust, vulnerability, and sharing emotions, among others. What happened when we were boys and we demonstrated these characteristics outwardly? How did our caregivers respond? How did our schoolmates respond? I absolutely believe that men want to connect with others, and that when they move to do so they are often stepping into their trauma, completely unaware. It happened to me every time with the women I let into my heart, including Nancy, who got through to me more than any other human being ever has. I would react. I would do a lot of the things from the signs of trauma listed above. I had no idea that it was about trauma and shame.

This is not about inviting men to do something they do not want to do. Larry said that one of the most important things he has learned about men in his years of recovery is that "given the chance, most men want to be vulnerable if it can lead to meaningful relationships and connection." I heard this from the men I interviewed over and over again—the importance of vulnerability (which I discuss at length in Chapter Eight) seemed to be at the crux of their healing. Men want this closeness, and so they unwittingly wade into the seemingly shallow waters of early intimacy and end up dropping off into the deep and turbulent whirlpools of trauma, unaware and unprepared. And many of us drown.

My physical growth problem burned into my consciousness the belief in my smallness and weakness. For decades I lived with a constant voice inside me that told me I was not a man. I didn't share that with anyone; it simply followed me wherever I went. I was mostly afraid of men. Okwas talked about the change in how he now sees men as a result of having dealt with the effects of trauma in his life for many years: "Men are not abusers; they are people I can open my heart to." That statement is huge, and the change it represents is monumental.

I hated weakness in others—men, women, or children. I would often have a strong emotional urge to destroy it. I wanted to destroy that which my father had tried to destroy in me. I hated it because I hated that wounded part of myself that I had turned my back on so many years ago. That is where the idea of complex trauma, a more layered trauma that represents multiple incidences of trauma over the course of time, comes in for so many of us. My father's violence and alcoholism created an environment where my issues and pain were invisible. My mother was struggling with her own life-threatening medical issues over the course of my time in high school, making it difficult for her to do anything other than survive, particularly in such an alcoholic home. It took me many years to even acknowledge how traumatic those experiences were for me, because it seemed like such a pathetic kind of trauma. So I dismissed it and the validity of the pain, and that is *precisely* how trauma is self-perpetuating. It is what I have watched man after man do in his life. As with many of you, my formative experiences defined the world of masculinity in which I lived. Many years later I found myself asking in a fairly profound way, *What does it mean to be a man who is in recovery and a child of an alcoholic/addict?* The core of my recovery from the effects of growing up in a violent alcoholic home has been attempting to develop a healthy and mature masculinity. Much of that has been trying to unlearn all of the ineffective and disconnecting behaviors I learned growing up in that environment.

There Is a Solution

Yes, there is a solution. The first step is breaking the silence. Those of us who have discovered the real impact of trauma on our lives need to speak up about it. We are growing in number as more and more treatment programs, mental health professionals, and other service providers are being trained in trauma and providing trauma-informed care. It is also imperative that we speak about it in our meetings, with the men we sponsor, and with all of the men we know and love. Every time I am invited to give any kind of recovery talk, I share it. I share loudly and as fearlessly and shamelessly as I can, even though sometimes my voice still shakes.

I was playing golf with Emilio, a friend and one of the men I interviewed, and as we were waiting for the rest of our foursome to arrive at the course, he said, "I've been following your blog, but I gotta tell you I just don't get this trauma stuff. I can't identify with it. That wasn't my experience." I wasn't sure where he was going with that, but he then began talking about one of the guys he sponsors. "There is something else going on with him and I can't help him. I really see that now. I don't think working the steps *more* is what he needs. It's something else. I think it's trauma."

Emilio is one of those guys who gets it, not because he has the background but because he listens with his heart to what people are saying. He appreciates and honors his limits. He and I have had multiple conversations about it from both a professional and a personal standpoint. He was visibly moved one day when I described some of my experiences growing up and some of the psychological struggles I had in my adolescence. With tears in *his* eyes, he said, "I'm so sorry that happened to you." I told him I'd be happy to talk to his sponsee, who may want to see a therapist trained in trauma. Okwas talked about the benefits of outside counseling in helping him heal from trauma: "Going inward instead of striking out at those around me and using the tools I learned in trauma counseling have helped me each time to get better and better at working through my trauma."

There are millions of men like Emilio's sponsee all over the world. They are being killed by their addiction as they attempt to exorcise the demons of trauma tearing them apart from inside. And then there are the multitudes of men in recovery, having worked so hard to slay the dragon of addiction only to realize there is another dragon that is just as destructive and tenacious. And it is heartbreaking, because men tend to cast long shadows, and that means more people get hurt.

The second part of the solution is getting the word out about our understanding of the science behind trauma and some incredibly effective interventions such as EMDR and EFT. Here are some tips you can begin to use immediately to help you deal with anxiety, intense emotion, any kind of dissociation, and just generally feeling "off" or "overwhelmed."

- Connecting with someone else—honestly, authentically, and vulnerably
- Meditating
- Getting an app for your smartphone or computer that plays relaxing sounds and/or music
- Deep breathing
- Visualization
- Counting (especially while taking slow breaths)
- Exercise
- Music (playing a musical instrument; listening to songs that you have an emotional connection to)
- Journaling
- Yoga

Into Action

There is no question that men's trauma is one of the most significant factors getting in the way of their relationships with others. I will continue to say it: Do not wait to deal with trauma. Seek out experts and see if there is trauma you need to address. If there is, do it. Be cautious of anyone who says they can clear up your trauma in four or five sessions. That may or may not be the case. Depending on the severity of the trauma, you can experience a significant reduction in your trauma-related symptoms. But more than likely, as with so many other things, it will be a journey, just like the rest of your recovery.

CHAPTER FOUR
Manly Feelings

"To feel is to be alive." —Ed

Creating and maintaining healthy relationships requires communication, and an essential part of communication involves recognizing, acknowledging, and expressing feelings. Continuing the analogy of this book as a map, you could say that feelings are the "true north" of a relationship. When we sense we are off course and are not sure where we are going, if we can notice what we feel in the situation, we will be able to better understand what is happening and the direction in which we need to go. Not feeling our feelings doesn't mean they don't exist. As Nate said, "Feelings are there whether or not we acknowledge them." The more intimate the relationship, the more feelings we experience and the more intense they are. Our feelings are a fundamental part of meaningfully connecting with our loved ones.

In the last few years, I have discovered an important fact. In recovery we talk about how feelings are not facts. This is true. Feelings are also genderless. What does that mean? Assigning gender to specific feelings is something I was guilty of in my first book, and is something that our culture does to boys and men starting at a very early age. It is part of the essence of the Water. Unintentionally, I perpetuated the idea that feelings such as hurt, sadness, and fear are feminine. But if men and women and boys and girls all have those feelings, how can they be masculine or feminine? Feelings are universal; they have no gender. You may not be aware of them right now because you have been trained through the Rules not to recognize them. And if you do recognize them, you are prohibited from acknowledging them to others. But as we continue to evolve as humans and grow in our recovery, we become more aware of all of our feelings. They are part of our life experience. As Ed said previously, "To feel is to be alive."

My challenge, and the challenge of a lot of the men I spoke with for this book, is accepting and expressing my feelings. How comfortable are you telling your partner that your feelings are hurt? I had specific patterns of interaction in my romantic relationships when the other person did something and my feelings were hurt. All I had to do was say, "That hurt my feelings," or "That hurt," or even simply say, "Ouch." Instead, how did I behave? First, I acted offended. Then, I began to raise my voice. I would attack them with criticism. Were they guilty? Absolutely, but mostly guilty of being human. I felt hurt and I could not bear to admit it. The discomfort and shame I felt would not allow me to simply hold the feeling. I would start a fight rather than admit my feelings were hurt. How many times have you done something similar?

What we are talking about here is vulnerability. Jim said that one of the most important things he has learned about being a man when it comes to having feelings is that "it is not only okay, but vital to be vulnerable." As easy as it is to say this, it is amazingly hard to practice. If you are like most men, you have been trained to not even realize when your feelings are hurt, let alone admit it. You've learned to hide your vulnerability. You do it with most everyone: your coworkers, friends, family, kids, and life partner.

The problem is that our feelings get hurt all the time, especially as men in recovery, since we tend to be a bit more sensitive than the average Joe. After decades of building circuitry that tells us hurt feelings are a sign of weakness and being less of a man, men don't feel or express hurt; we lose touch with the very real experience of being hurt. We cannot rewire our brains overnight. We cover it up. We hide from it and deny it. But it is there. In recovery the Rules are turned on their head. As Hugh stated,

"Sharing feelings is a sign of strength, not weakness." But you have to believe that at your core to make it part of your truth.

The Man Rules have convinced us that feeling hurt is a weakness associated with girls and women. That is what we are told in different ways by our parents, schoolyard friends, the media, and others. Sometimes this message is explicit, but it is also embedded in our culture, our books and movies, and our songs and folktales. We typically hide men's hurt, sadness, fear, and insecurity, while honoring and even exalting those same feelings in women. Sometimes, with the best of intentions, our fathers and even our mothers tried to toughen us up and protect us from being beaten up by the world. We grow up telling ourselves if we are going to be stronger or manlier we cannot allow our feelings to be hurt, or to feel sadness or fear, or to share our insecurities.

The problem with such posturing is that it's all bullshit. If you are a human being who cares about others, you will feel hurt from time to time. You cannot avoid it. You can pretend it is not there, but it doesn't prevent the experience from happening. The bind is that if feeling hurt is for girls and women, and I am a man and want to be seen as and feel like a man, then I cannot allow myself to be hurt or acknowledge it. So, as is the case with the Rules a lot of the time, in order to be a man I must sacrifice my humanity.

Freedom comes when we realize that feeling hurt is just feeling hurt, and it has nothing to do with gender and everything to do with ego. We need to feel it and let it go—"name it, face it, trace it, and erase it" is a common saying in recovery. I would amend that saying to "name it, face it, trace it, and *embrace* it." And let it go. If we learn to embrace what we are feeling, it is so much easier for our feelings to simply pass through us. As men we spend a lot of our time fighting our feelings and the shame we feel for having them, thereby making the experience much more difficult than it needs to be.

Can you be present with the emotion of fear? If you are anything like me, the interpretation of my fear through a shamed-based Man Rules lens calling me a wimp and telling me I'm weak happens in a split second. It is just fear. It means nothing about you (or me) as a man. If you do not consciously step in and acknowledge fear, chances are the negative judgments and repression of the feeling will rule the day. Mike talked about it this way: "Feelings are a part of who I am, and they are not to be denied. I have to acknowledge fear in order to connect with what's really going on." Acknowledging it openly takes away some of the power it may have over us.

The danger in speaking against the Rules like this is that you might think I am trying to turn men into women. That would be most unfortunate; however, it is also to be expected because that is the way men are socialized and effectively trained. When the Rules are operating, we don't see them. As I described earlier, they are the Water in which we swim, and we often aren't aware of them and their effects on us. They keep us enslaved, and we lash out against anyone who threatens to pull the veil back. A young man I met at a training in Kansas aptly stated, "We cannot let the Rules rule us." We then come to find that the true measure of a man is one who can be his true self in the face of others who may not be able to honor that. It's a simple truth. As Bob said, "Other men will judge you; it matters less and less." It takes so much energy to be constantly fighting against who we are. Earl said it well: "Authenticity, being a fully present man, is wonderful and easier than not."

Of course, these are only some of the feelings that have been all but eliminated from men's experience of life. As a result of this emotional castration, many men walk around with incredible amounts of grief and loss, carrying the pain like a bag of rocks everywhere they go, and adding more to the bag over the years. I will talk more about grief in Chapter Thirteen, Healing Trauma.

The Anger Funnel

Think about all of the feelings we can experience as human beings. Now, imagine all of those feelings going into a funnel and coming out the narrow bottom as some form of anger. Our depth and breadth of experiencing life gets compressed. The idea is that anger is often a secondary emotion. Think about the above discussion on the feelings of hurt and fear. As men we are trained to take many of the "softer" emotions (the emotions of vulnerability) and place them into a funnel. After these feelings are "edited" by the Man Rules, they often come out as some form of anger.

Anger Funnel

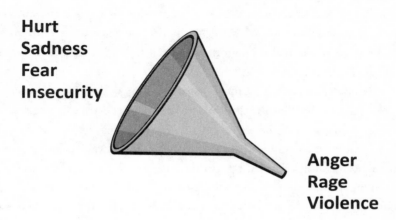

Hurt
Sadness
Fear
Insecurity

Anger
Rage
Violence

For the longest time when I was feeling hurt, sadness, insecurity, fear, or shame, I would often not even recognize those emotions, but rather would jump right into various forms of anger. I was not even aware I was responding that way. The last thing I was going to do was admit that I was feeling sad. Or hurt. Or insecure. Especially to Nancy. All of those feelings leave me feeling exposed and vulnerable. They are not "manly." Underneath my anger I had a sense there was something else going on, but I was not sure what it was. I certainly did not think it was because I was hurt or afraid. I didn't make the connection to my anger. Most men don't. The shame of having those feelings keeps you from acknowledging them. There is much less shame in a man being angry than in appearing "weak."

So long as you are a slave to the Man Rules, you will never master the anger funnel. If we cannot learn how to master the anger funnel, our relationships will not survive. What man wants to admit that his feelings have been hurt? Or that he is afraid? He doesn't want his man card to be revoked. But good luck for that same man trying to have a real and intimate relationship with a partner. That is the bind that confronts so many men. Of course, some men have found partners just as wounded as they are who had put up with men who were shut down or angry because it kept the couples dance alive; both partners had excuses to be unhappy and could easily blame each other. What a hard and sad way to live. Why would you work so hard to recover from a miserable condition of life such as addiction, only to accept a low-grade misery in your relationships?

Once a man decides, as most recovering men do, that he wants a healthy relationship with real intimacy, he is screwed if he is not willing to redefine how the Rules fit in his life. He must learn to wear them as a loose garment as opposed to a straitjacket. He always has the option of being an asshole (from subtle to downright abusive) and hurting the person he professes to love so he doesn't have to feel vulnerable. As men in recovery we are constantly confronted with the impact of our behavior, encouraged to invest in our relationships, and taught how to do it better by other men. We learn to be more open and honest about who we are and what we value. Intellectually, most of us would tell you that we would choose vulnerability and trust, but when we're in that moment, feeling the overwhelming force of the Rules pushing us toward one direction, it is a lot harder to do.

We need to be challenged to be our best selves. Screw being a man according to anyone else's definition. Be who you are! If you show up genuine and honest in your most intimate relationships, you will experience a depth of love and trust you never felt possible. But it takes a real man to do that kind of work. Jose said it beautifully: "In recovery, I value the relationships that I have in my life. I'm constantly learning how to nurture the healthy ones and set better boundaries in the unhealthy ones. Some of the people in my life have not changed one bit since I got sober nine and a half years ago, but I have, and that has made all the difference."

Into Action

▶ When was the last time your feelings were hurt? What happened? What was your part? How did you act? What feelings did you express to the person? How did you let that person know that your feelings were hurt? If you did not, why not? Now answer the same questions for the last time you felt: afraid, sad, insecure, lonely, and ashamed.

▶ Make a commitment. The next time your significant other or someone else with whom you are close hurts your feelings, take a deep breath and admit it to him or her. See what happens. *You can try this when you feel afraid, sad, lonely, and insecure as well.*

CHAPTER FIVE
Creating Healthy Relationships

"My relationships have become more conscious, intimate, and loving; they are still the greatest teacher and reflection for me." –Sean

This chapter could be likened to a compass. It gives us direction and helps us to locate ourselves on the map, particularly in relation to others. It also helps us know better what direction we want to move in. I believe that most men have good intentions when they get into romantic relationships. It is not just about getting laid, or trying to find someone to take care of them. Child psychologist and trauma expert Dr. Bruce Perry talks about our brains and how we are *all* wired for connection and relationship. Our need for connection is rooted deep inside our DNA. Despite the negative stereotypes about men and even some of our behavior, our natural inclination is to connect. Men are not the relational aberrations that we are often made out to be.

The Rules imply it is unmanly to admit that we value our relationships and want to connect with others, or that, God forbid, we need others in our lives. Yet there is an incredibly rich and rapidly growing chorus of scientists, psychologists, quantum physicists, sociologists, and others who are finding irrefutable evidence for how human beings are intended to connect to one another.

Relationships are central to the twelve-step recovery process. Nate talked about it this way: "In recovery, I learned how to make commitments and stick with them. Although it's not always easy, I have learned to hang in there through the rough times, to engage in problem solving, honest conversation, and conflict management. I have been able to remain in a twenty-one-year marriage and have helped raise two children. I try to work the steps in all areas of my life, not the least of which is in my own home." If you think about it, every step has something to do with relationships. Think about what a recovery meeting is: a place where we come from our busy lives that are often disconnected from others' and have the chance to take off our masks and be real. It's an environment in which we are constantly learning how to have relationships.

It ain't rocket science, but it is consistent with brain science: A primary solution to one of the world's most destructive and baffling illnesses consists of people sitting around talking about who they really are and how they are really doing? That is why so many of us who once felt like we *had* to go to meetings in order to be okay now *want* to go. It feeds our souls. Every human being wants this same kind of connection. Science has even recently identified the chemical oxytocin that produces a pleasurable feeling when we experience love, bonding, and connection, reinforcing the value of the connection and our need for it.

In one of the trainings Rick and I do for clinicians we have a breakout exercise entitled "A House Divided," where the participants are invited to share aspects of the outside of their house (their outer self) and the inside of their house (their inner self). They are asked which aspects of each part of their house they would like to keep and which they would like to discard. On one occasion, two men—both of whom were in twelve-step recovery for multiple decades—who have worked together for over a decade talked about how the exercise got them to open up, connect at a level they had never connected at before, and share things about themselves that they never really knew about each other. They both remarked how special that was for them. This experience clarifies that if we are not intentional about our relationships, it is far too easy to confine them to the surface of what is possible, even when we have all of the tools we need to have deeper and more intimate connections.

Dr. Perry also talks about what has been happening to the quality of our relationships and our brains over the last two hundred years as technology has moved us toward greater isolation and disconnection. It is a lot easier to go down into the man cave and turn on *SportsCenter* than talk to our partner about how hard our day was or how we are feeling disconnected in our relationship with him or her. The ability to check out and isolate is not gender specific. One of the ways that women can check out of relationships is by focusing on what their partner is or isn't doing. Or they do some of the stereotypical things that women are known to do, like go shopping. Or read romance novels or watch soaps. Or do whatever it is that helps them to check out. They can be just as constrained by the set of Rules that pertain to women.

We don't truly see each other much of the time because we see what we want (or what we don't want). We become means to each other's ends. How often do I take the time to really connect with the woman selling the juice at the airport, the man at the ticket counter, or the person sitting next to me on the plane? Sometimes I do a little experiment and I stop and ask someone who is working a register how their day is going. When they say the robotic "Good" or "Fine," I look at them and say, "Really, how is your day going?" I smile or do something to let them know I am seriously interested, and sometimes they respond. Other times they repeat what they said. Of course, I am often guilty of doing the same. My point is that it takes time and a conscious effort to be present and really connect with others. Through our actions, we can teach others how to be with us.

We are so often not known to each other because we are not known to ourselves. Sure, many of us can talk a good game. The inundation of self-help banter in our media and society as a whole has led a lot of us to believe that if we can spout this stuff, it means we are living it. This is always a danger in the recovery community. I speak from years of painful lack of self-awareness. I could sound so good. I knew exactly what to say. In my work as a counselor at a treatment center, I knew what to say to you about the quality of your relationships and what you needed to do to improve them. I'd tell you how you were failing yourself and your loved ones because of your selfish behavior. Then I would leave our session, call my girlfriend because she had been traveling and I had not heard from her, and proceed to get into a fight because of my own neediness and fear. I was addicted to the cycle of needing to feel wanted, followed by feeling rejected, acting poorly, and ultimately feeling ashamed of my behavior. And the more shame I felt, the needier I became. Talk about self-defeating patterns of behavior. I could wax philosophic about any number of things. I was "deep." But to sit still and actually feel life? And to be okay with whatever it was that I was experiencing at an emotional level? For there to be a congruence between what was going on in my head and in my heart? That is a part of the journey which, in all honesty, I am just beginning to truly experience.

For years now, certain putative relationship experts have been calling men on the carpet on national TV and in best sellers for how we act in our relationships and our overall lack of relational competence. But what I almost never see is these folks looking at the man and saying, "You know, Dan, I understand that nobody sat you down and told you how to do these things. I understand that you are doing everything you have been taught to do. I believe there is a part of you that really wants to do things differently." No, they are happy to put on a show, shaming these men, and playing to the anger and hurt of the women in the audience, with little true respect for either the men or the women. Rarely have I seen a genuine compassion and love in these so-called relationship experts' diatribes against men. Why is that? It is a lot easier to complain about men's disengagement from our relationships than it is to attempt to understand where it comes from and what else might be going on.

Let's face it: In our society in general, it is not cool for guys to go around asking for help from each other in their relationships with others. You don't often see a lot of men sitting around talking about their relationships and asking each other for support because of the particular struggle they are having—not because they are not struggling or because they do not care, but because the Rules prohibit it. That prohibition is lessening, but it remains strong. Can you imagine a bunch of guys muting the TV at halftime of an NFL game to check in with each other about the status of their relationships and what is working and what is not working? It could look something like this:

Dan: "Hey guys, so I know I checked in with you during the playoffs two weeks ago."

Guy #1: "Yeah, how are you and Nancy doing? How have you been doing with the fear?"

Guy #2: "I would really like to know, because Alice and I have been going through the same thing and it has been really hard."

Dan: "Well, I have to tell you. I talked to her that night about what we had discussed, and it made a huge difference. She was a bit put off at first, but I did just like you guys suggested and held her hand while I spoke to her. That seemed to make all of the difference."

Guy #1: "I knew it! Sheila was the same way when I talked to her that time. It was hard, but it made such a difference. The funny thing is that it felt just as good to me!"

Guy #2: "Okay. I am going to try it too."

Guy #3: (*walking in from the bathroom, sitting down, and not sure what is going on*) "Uh . . . could someone pass the chips?"

How likely is that to happen? Instead, the Rules often stipulate that one guy complains about his "old lady" and other men say something like "She's a woman, what do you expect? Just say 'yes, dear' and move on." Laugh and crack open another beer. Or congratulate yourselves for being so wise because you're in recovery.

However, if you were to sit with us men in recovery and listen to us, you would hear that a lot of what we talk about *is* our relationships. Why? Because in the recovery community the Rules are different. First, recovery gives us the ability to be in relationships—something that was not possible when we were active in our addiction.

Roland talked about it this way: "Without recovery I was never able to be present 100 percent in any relationship except the one I had with my drugs. Everyone and everything else came second or third. Today, I can be the father, husband, or friend I was never capable of being in my active addiction." We have the chance to achieve emotional recovery, which, said simply, is when our recovery moves from our head to our heart. The program becomes something we truly begin to practice in all of our relationships.

Recovery gives us the opportunity to step into our true selves. And our truest selves are the ones who want to connect and be in relationship with others. Recovery is about asking for help, admitting we do not know, and being authentic about our inner lives. As Bob said, "We not only get to bring the truth of who we are into those relationships, but we also get to discover the truth of who we are in those relationships." What an incredible gift. Learning how to be in healthy and meaningful relationships with others is discussed throughout the literature of recovery, be it in Overeaters Anonymous (OA), Alcoholics Anonymous (AA), Narcotics Anonymous (NA), Sex and Love Addicts Anonymous (SLAA), Al-Anon, Gamblers Anonymous (GA), or any other twelve-step group. Don't get me wrong; the Rules are still powerful forces in our psyche, but they do not dominate us the way they tend to in the larger culture. That "relaxed masculinity" makes it safe for us to be more honest about our feelings and what is happening in our lives. If you are not experiencing at least some of that sense of safety and permission to be vulnerable in your recovery meetings, then you want to look at what might be holding you back, and if you determine it to be the culture of the meeting as opposed to your own fear and isolation, you need to consider finding another group of recovering men. We are out there.

Male Relational Dread

For almost forty years now, a growing group of men within many of the social science fields have been looking at the psychological and relational needs of men. Only in the past two decades have larger fields of thought begun to take notice of these developing theories and practices. This is due in part to the Columbine and other school shootings. The scandals within the Catholic Church and at Penn State University focused attention on one of the greatest taboos of men's experience: sexual abuse. Almost all of this work has been informed by a feminist critique of gender roles. One theory I have discovered, thanks to mentors like Stephanie Covington, PhD, that has been important to my work is Relational Cultural Theory (RCT).

Relational Cultural Theory emphasizes the importance of relationships in the development of an individual's sense of self. RCT recognizes that power, socialization, and cultural norms and values play a pivotal role in our ability to connect and stay in connection with one another. In 1978, Jean Baker-Miller, MD, along with three psychologists, Judith Jordan, Irene Striver, and Janet Surrey, posited that developmental psychology and clinical practice were not models that worked well for women and their experiences. They focused on exploring the qualities of relationships that foster healthy growth in women, not necessarily realizing that this developmental model spoke to a common human experience, even if it was experienced differently by men and women.

Because Relational Cultural Theory was primarily focused on women and women's experience, very little had been written on this subject until Stephen Bergman, MD, a Harvard-trained psychiatrist and Janet Surrey's spouse, wrote a seminal article on men and RCT. Bergman acknowledges that men are raised to want independence and individuation, but he says there is also a significant cost in our lack of connection and participation in relationships that are not mutually supportive or empowering.

Men are raised to separate and be separate, irrespective of the harm that does to themselves or others. Control and power are two of the main tools through which boys are encouraged to develop into men. There is little about our corrupt ideas regarding power and control that nourishes our relationships and helps us to be authentic and loving human beings. Of course, that does not mean there is anything wrong with wanting to have power or control. As my coauthor of *Helping Men Recover,* training partner and colleague Rick Dauer says, "The desire for personal power and control is a normal and healthy human drive. It is the tactics that far too many men employ, such as manipulation, intimidation, and violence, that are problematic." True personal power is a function of connection, respect, and mutuality.

The challenge for men is overcoming years of socialization that reinforce separateness, isolation, emotional illiteracy, and varying degrees of relational incompetence. When men get into intimate relationships and find their partners wanting, even begging for, communication, vulnerability, and openness, they often freeze up in fear. Bergman has labeled this "male relational dread." This dread manifests differently depending on the man's past experiences, temperament, and relational competence.

If men and women both want and need relationships and if relationships require similar things from men and women—connection, authenticity, emotional openness, and vulnerability—then maybe we aren't as different as has been purported. Maybe differences between men and women are not nearly as stark or as rigid as previously thought. Like I said earlier, maybe we aren't from different planets after all.

So again, what are the qualities of a healthy relationship? Some of them are as follows:

- Intimacy
- Honesty
- Vulnerability
- Trust
- Partnership
- Sharing emotions
- Compromise
- Healthy conflict

Which of those elements are part of the Man Rules? None of them. The one that an argument could be made for is honesty, but not if honesty includes emotional honesty. If men are told directly or indirectly that these qualities are not manly and are to be avoided, if we are not taught how to develop them, then how could we possibly be expected to know how to practice them?

If we view having a relationship through the perspective of building strength by lifting weights, most of us have little to no muscle or strength to be in relationships. That also means we can't go into a relationship expecting or being expected to bench-press 200 pounds right off the bat. As embarrassing as it might be, we may even have to start with just the fifty-pound bar. Are you man enough to do that? The truth is that we have to build our relationship muscles, and this takes time and a lot of practice.

Into Action

▶ Talk to your partner about your relationship and ask him or her, on a scale of 1 to 10, how well you are doing. Ask specifically:
  • What are the three best things you are doing?
  • What are three things you could improve?

▶ Think about your three most important relationships in your life. For each one, answer the following:
  • What are three things you did to nurture the relationship?
  • What are three things you did to create disconnection?
  • What did you learn from that relationship that has helped you in other relationships? How does it relate to the Man Rules?
  • What is something you did in that relationship that has negatively impacted other relationships? How does it relate to the Man Rules?

CHAPTER SIX
Staying in Healthy Relationships

"Without recovery I have no real relationships." —Mark

The ability to help create healthy relationships is vital, but we also have to learn how to stay in those relationships and keep them supportive and loving. If the previous chapter was about learning where we need to go, then this chapter focuses on what to do when we get there.

Although they may not be especially healthy, many men have no problem *getting into* relationships. We get into relationships easily—with women. The Rules tell us we should not be gay, or even get too close to men emotionally. We are supposed to pursue heterosexual relationships. According to the Man Rules, our ability to get laid validates us, and if having to get into a relationship makes that happen or if it happens as a result, so be it. The Rules also tell women that they are validated when someone chases after them. Men are further validated when we can "chase down" a woman and "win" her over. She is a statement that tells us and others that we are real men.

Even for those men who do not identify as heterosexual, women still play a critical role. No man goes on this journey of life without women playing a key part. Our responsibility is to work on coming to peace with women, which means coming to peace with our mothers and their imperfections, recognizing how we devalue so much of what we associate with girls and women. As a society, we have to start talking honestly about women and stop the foolish implication that they can't be just as destructive to relationships as men, or that they are inherently relationship experts.

Let me be clear: I love women. My daughter, my wife, my good female friends, all of the women in my family, and all of the incredibly powerful women who have changed and are changing the world whom I have had the privilege to know and even work with have been great gifts. There are amazing women all over the world whom I will never know and who are helping to change the world in wonderful ways and standing against the injustices that girls and women continue to face.

At no point will you hear me saying that men and women are the same or that we should be. When it comes to our relationships with women, the challenge is how we honor our gender-based differences, respect and give them equal value for women and men, without using our differences as an excuse to ignore what we have in common. I know that once I stopped worshiping and fearing women, I began to see how beautifully wounded they are—just like us men.

Women have the burden of their own Rules to follow. Here are some of the Woman Rules:

1. Always look beautiful.
2. Your weight determines your worth.
3. Be passive.
4. Assume responsibility for taking care of the house.

Into Action

Take a few minutes to come up with as many additional Woman Rules as you can.

How do the Woman Rules compare to the Man Rules?

What are some of the Rules that seem restrictive to women? How so? What are some of the Rules that affirm the best in women? How so?

Do you see some of the challenges that women have? Do you see some of the double binds? Bobby talked about what has happened as a result of his being able to "see" women: "I try to see what many view as weaknesses to be strengths, to see intuition and nurturing as God-given strengths, not personal shortcomings to be exploited." If you have not already shared your list of Woman Rules with a woman in your life, do so now and get some feedback from her about the list you came up with. Ask her and perhaps some other women what is missing. Ask them about what it is like for them.

Staying in relationships is quite a bit tougher than getting into them. Staying in intimate relationships requires us to face ourselves in a way that we are not used to. We may not even feel equipped to do so. The Rules have taught us how not to be in relationships. If and when we actually commit to a relationship, the Rules may influence us to feel miserable in that relationship, leading us to destroy it. A lot of men tend to be "runners." At a certain point in a relationship our response is to shut down and walk or run away, to escape. Why do we run? Because we do not know how to handle the emotional intensity that comes from a healthy and intimate relationship.

We aren't aware this is why we're running. Instead, we come up with some other reason—something is wrong with our partner, the honeymoon period is over, it just isn't "right," or we may feel inherently relationally deficient. Perhaps we avoid getting too close by engaging in serial sexual relationships, one after another. A lot of it has to do with the fact that we so often have no idea what we are feeling. But remember, we come by it honestly. Since the day we were born we have been told most feelings are not okay. Feelings are not manly. All we really get to own is anger, and that is not the ideal emotion for getting close to someone and creating intimacy.

1 + 1 = 3

When I was in graduate school, at the urging of a good friend I enrolled in a human sexuality course. Other than the fairly rudimentary and brief "sex ed" I received in high school and the miseducation I received through far too many hours of pornography and colluding with other men in our sexual bravado, I had no in-depth understanding of sexuality. I was twenty-four years old when I took that class. Although I had had sex with women, I did not have a clue about my sexuality or their sexuality. I thought sex and sexuality were basically synonymous. Suffice it to say that by the end of that class I had a whole new appreciation for my body, a woman's body, and the vastness of the idea of sexuality. I discuss this further in Chapter Ten.

One concept that class introduced me to is $1 + 1 = 3$. In short, when two people are in a relationship there are actually three entities, the two individuals and the relationship. Still relatively new in my recovery, I continued to be under the trance of Hollywood's "you complete me" formula that says $\frac{1}{2} + \frac{1}{2} = 1$. Most of us grow up with this image, and it is a lie.

The way this lie affects us is that it reinforces the idea that women are responsible for the emotional part of the relationship. That is the "half" they bring, while men supposedly bring the "logical" and "rational" half. The main message is that others complete us, and that without them we are left incomplete. This lie also means that men don't have to focus on developing the qualities that women are supposed to bring to the relationship, and vice versa. Very few people will thrive in a relationship like this because it feels so limiting—it is predicated on deficits rather than strengths.

The problem is that much of our misery and pain comes from within. Marty said, "I took a year and a half off to feel better in my own skin before moving forward in a relationship." In the discussion of Step Ten, AA's *Twelve Steps and Twelve Traditions* states, "It is a spiritual axiom that whenever we are disturbed, no matter what the cause, it is because there is something wrong with us." The first time I heard that I could only come up with one word: ouch. That idea flew in the face of everything I thought up until that point, that is, other people and the rest of the world were the sources of my discomfort. How could it have anything to do with *me*? It is important for us to do our own personal work before we can create and maintain a healthy, serious relationship.

When we take the time to get to know ourselves, and put time and attention into preparing ourselves to be in a healthy relationship, we are able to attract more supportive and healthy partners. I have spent many a night in great emotional turmoil after an argument with Nancy meditating on that question, because I do believe that spiritual axiom mentioned above: It has nothing to do with her. I believe it is always true, and if I can stay with that I can find and soothe the wound inside me that needs to be healed. Of course, that is much easier said than done.

In fact, I had one of the most amazing, powerful, and vulnerable experiences of my life as a result of practicing that axiom. I had gone to sleep one night feeling very emotional and wanting so much to project it onto Nancy, even though I knew it wasn't about her. I knew it was something that was happening inside me and I needed to simply stay with the feeling. I couldn't sleep, so I went downstairs into the guest room and lay there. I began to pray, "Please let me feel this." It has been so hard for me to simply allow myself to feel. I lay there pleading with God to help me just to feel. I knew I had this overwhelming feeling of sadness and it was stuck inside me. "Help me to give myself permission to have my tears. I want them back."

When I was fifteen I stood in front of the mirror, tired of crying myself to sleep night after night, feeling abandoned by my family and by God. I looked angrily and dismissively at myself in the reflection and I said, "You will never cry again. You will not feel sad. Never again!" And I was successful, even through the deaths of five family members in six years, including my father, and our losses while trying to have a child. Over the course of two and half decades I had shed very few tears.

That night I felt the sadness rising inside me. I prayed and took deep breaths as I lay in bed, trying to unclench my teeth, which felt as if they had been glued shut. I started to have a feeling as if I were about to get sick. I was so tired of having my inability to cry destroy my happiness and separate me from my wife and daughter and others. I felt the smallest tears coming. I summoned them from the depth of my being. "Please, God . . ." I lay there for thirty minutes in this state of limbo. And then I got up and walked upstairs. Nancy heard me coming up the stairs and I was walking toward her and she said, still asleep, "Dan, what is going on?" I couldn't talk, as I felt the grief rising inside me about to erupt. "Dan, what is the matter? What is going on?" She could hear me breathing shallowly as I approached the bed. I simply collapsed in the bed into her arms. And I began to cry. To wail. I felt it in the depths of my soul. I struggled to breathe as she held me. I cried for an hour.

And then we heard the footsteps coming up the stairs. It was our daughter, Grace. I thought to myself, *No way . . . I cannot let Grace see me like this.* I said to Nancy, through the sobbing, "No, don't let her come up. Have her go back." And then, as quickly as I said it, I knew that Grace *had* to be there. This was the missing piece. This was how we break the cycle as men, when we let our children see our undisguised vulnerability. Grace walked over to the bed, also still half asleep. She got into bed with us. She was trying to figure out what was going on. "Mommy, why is Daddy crying?" I surrendered to the fact that she was there and continued to let the grief come. It seemed endless. Grace instinctively got in between us and lay with us. I felt her tiny arm lying across my stomach. She said, "Mommy, what is wrong with Daddy?" She was three and she had never seen me cry.

"Daddy is sad, honey."

"Why is he sad?"

"He is just sad, honey. Just like you and Mommy get sad, Daddy gets sad too." My heart smiled as I heard Nancy saying this.

And then Grace got closer to me, moved her arm from my stomach, and began rubbing my head lightly. "There, there . . . there, there . . . it's okay. It's okay, Daddy." I was so moved I cried even more. I felt her pulling me closer with her arm. She was rubbing my head and my face. I felt so comforted by this precious little three-year-old. She then said to Nancy, "Should we read Daddy a book?"

"Yes, honey, that is a wonderful idea."

I lay there being comforted by these two amazing people. Grace got out of bed and went and got a book. It was a book about ten caterpillars. She started going through the book, one page at a time. It started with ten caterpillars, then nine, then eight, all the way until there was only one. And then she turned the page and all of the caterpillars had turned into butterflies. Of all the books she could have chosen, she chose that book. I laughed, pulled her close to me, and kissed her, and the three of us lay in bed together.

This story came as a result of me practicing the principles I have been learning for almost two decades. As a result, I have made a significant step in breaking the cycle of trauma in my family and have showed my little girl that men do cry, and that strength, power, and courage can show up in a lot of ways. Of equal importance, I showed myself that I could do it. I could show the depths of my vulnerability, be with Nancy, and be present with the pain.

I would love to report that since that experience I have not swallowed my pain, or taken it out on Grace or Nancy, but that is not the case. As much work as I've done, the Rules still run deep inside me. But there has been an undeniable shift in how I show up in my life. My recovery has definitely been enriched and brought to a new level. The greatest part of this story for you, the reader, is that I am not special. I have no special power or insight into life that is not also available to you. I know that some of you reading this are already far along this road and this is merely validation for the way you have been living. We must put this message out to counteract the negative and demeaning messages about men and our relational competencies that still abound in our society. We can't just change what men think; we have to change what we think about men.

Hang in There

Having just celebrated ten years of marriage, I feel strongly about this section. It's sad that for my generation ten years of marriage is seen as a long time. I joke that it is the new silver anniversary. But when and under what circumstances is it the right time to end a relationship? I do not pretend it is an easy decision. I do believe, however, that a lot of good relationships end unnecessarily. In one year I watched four friends either get divorced or resolve to divorce. Each of the past several years I have watched friends get divorced. Most of them were married for fewer than five years, some for more than ten years, and two for over twenty years.

Each partner has to be willing to stare into the abyss and ask the question, "Am I happy in my relationship?" And you must be prepared to take responsibility for your part. As Guy said, "It is not a 50/50 deal; it is a 100/100 deal. Both partners are always 100 percent responsible for the relationship." That does not mean there won't be times when one will carry more of the weight than the other, because that will happen.

Some of the men I know in recovery go through their relationships emotionally disconnected, acting out, unable to talk to their spouses about what they are feeling or why they are unhappy, and it festers. This is frequently a legacy of the Rules. What I have noticed is that a lot of us tend to continue to operate this way long into our recovery, with little appreciation for how much our behavior is affecting our loved ones. It certainly was true in my case. I cannot overemphasize, though, how much I believe that undiagnosed, untreated trauma is a root cause of this disconnection and acting out for so many of us. While it is no excuse for our behavior, it is important information to have as it helps us understand that we are not bad people, nor are we crazy.

I have to wonder how many men (and women) of my generation and younger really have a sense of what it takes to create a lasting relationship. I did not have the skills when I got into my first long-term relationship, or when I met my wife, or even well into our marriage. I had no idea what it really took to be married. If my wonderful wife had not previously been married, I doubt she would have known either. In recovery we talk about the five-year surrender. At about five years a man has an opportunity to take his recovery deeper and gain the emotional grounding necessary to live a more stable and fulfilling life. There clearly seems to be something similar happening in our most intimate partnerships. The proverbial "seven-year itch" is nothing more than an opportunity for both partners to surrender more deeply to the commitment they have made to one another. Like Ray said, "Growth comes only through struggle; embrace the struggle." There is something to be said for simply settling into the struggle and understanding it is part of the process.

It seems that my generation and those that follow have two opposing forces working within us in our efforts to have fulfilling relationships. One is the incredible "happiness entitlement" so many of us have, and the other is our genuine interest in having connected and meaningful relationships. We want to do things differently than so many of our parents who grew up with the ½ + ½ = 1 formula did them. When I first heard the 1+ 1 = 3 formula, I knew that was what I wanted. However, wanting something is not nearly enough when it comes to creating a loving and healthy relationship. As Allen Berger, PhD, says, "Desire does not equal ability." But wanting something meaningful is a good starting point. Our sincere desire to travel to Greece is wonderful, and it helps to create a vision of the place we would like to get to, but unless we save the money, investigate where to visit, look into airfare and accommodations, and take other concrete steps, it isn't more than fantasy. We may have the map of Greece and all of its beautiful islands right in front of us, but that does not get us to Greece.

As I mentioned earlier, the last thing Earnie Larsen said to me shortly before he died after I told him about this book was "Dan, it is pretty simple. A relationship will only work and will only last if both people are willing to do the work—the work to nurture the relationship and their own personal work. Period." It's so simple, yet it is some of the hardest counsel to follow. It is so much easier to blame someone else for our unhappiness. We still suffer from the delusion that our painful feelings are someone else's fault and we have no control over how we react.

Most of the men and women of my generation are not interested in the kind of relationships we watched previous generations have. These were usually relationships in which unresolved conflicts lingered, vulnerable thoughts and feelings were not shared, communication was like pulling teeth, and marriage was an obligation to be suffered through. Of course, if that is what we grew up with and we were not taught anything different, then what are the chances that just because we don't want to do our relationships that way, we won't have the end result? Not very good. Healthy relationships require dedication and hard work. We cannot learn to speak French fluently just because we want to. If nobody taught us French and spoke French around us when we were growing up, and we have had little practice in speaking the language, it will take a lot of work and discipline to become fluent. That is what it is like for men in relationships. People often expect us to speak French, and all we know how to say is *bonjour, merci,* and *au revoir.*

Gently Standing Up

One of the great challenges I have had, particularly as someone who has suffered from so much anger and shame, has been how to stand up to women. Perhaps the better term is asserting myself or setting healthy boundaries, but for a lot of men it may feel like standing up to women. Because women often feel powerless relative to men, they sometimes attempt to assert power where they can or where they think they have to. I am amazed at how many men are pushed around by the women in their lives. The women frequently cannot even see it, and justify their behavior by complaining about the man. The key is being able to take care of oneself and set healthy boundaries without being aggressive or abusive. That is the delicate path men have to learn to walk. This is what I mean by "gently standing up."

It seems silly, but every man knows how some women can trigger something inside him that results in him feeling like a lost little boy. For those of us who identify as heterosexual, our female spouses can have this effect because they are the ones to whom we get closest and let into the deepest parts of who we are. We also tend to invest a lot of our sense of self-worth in their approval. I know that many of my struggles with Nancy have come out of my shame being triggered when she is stating any number of things, but the message I hear (read: make up) is "You're not a man. You're less of a man. You're not a good man." It all seems to go back to feeling like less than a man. As Brené Brown has so wonderfully put it, men don't want to look weak in front of women, especially *our* women.

It is not often the case that we speak honestly about the fear we have of women and their opinions about us. Nate talked about the importance of "learning to take criticism and guidance from women." Josh talked about how important it has been to be truly vulnerable with the women in his life and how the biggest thing that has changed in the way he relates to women is "being open and allowing myself to be hurt." There is that word again: *vulnerable*. Josh went on to say, "I have learned how to stay open and have made a commitment to letting women, especially my spouse, see me." When we allow women to truly see us, it means we are stepping outside of the Man Rules. There is no way to be authentic and still be confined within the Rules.

I know many men who have been hurt deeply by a woman's sharp tongue, emotional neglect or unavailability, or other unhealthy behaviors women can bring into a relationship, including physical and sexual abuse. Men tend to think that women are supposed to be our safe haven, but they are just as flawed and human as men.

We have to learn how to set healthy boundaries with the women in our lives. They might have a hard time with it at first. It is all about the communication. We get to speak up, challenge double standards in expectations or behavior, and let the women in our lives know that we get to have a voice regarding the emotional health of the relationship. That means we need women who are willing to admit when they are wrong, to own their own shame, and to let go of any need to control. We get to ask for what we need, not demand it.

When we learn how to gently stand up to our partners, we are honoring their strength and our belief in the strength of the foundation of our relationship. We are stepping up in the relationship and saying, effectively, "You are not married to a boy who you have to caretake; you are married to a man, a partner, who is equally invested in the emotional health of the relationship."

Men can grow up with some pretty challenging and warped ideas about women based upon two primary experiences they can have in childhood: (1) having an abusive (emotionally, physically, sexually, and/or verbally) mother or mother figure, and/or (2) the pain and abandonment that many boys feel when they experience severe abuse from a father or father figure because of a mother's lack of willingness or inability to act and protect them. Add to this how a boy views his mother being treated by his father and the other men in her life and the messages he takes on, often subconsciously, from this. These are very powerful and formative experiences in how men view girls and women, and these experiences affect men long into their relationships, often without them having any awareness of it. And men do not often talk about them.

Why Won't You Talk to Me?

Normally when you see a section heading like this you expect it to be about a woman trying to get her man to open up, or it is some "expert" talking about how men are emotionally shut down and don't really know how to talk about their feelings. In this case, it is about men who get into recovery, get in touch with their inner lives, and want to have partners who are willing and able to do the same. I have seen over and over again situations in which men who have a fairly high degree of emotional awareness struggle with partners who refuse to get counseling, go to couples counseling, or acknowledge her (or his) part in the relationship that is not working.

When the relationship has endured a man's active addiction, the man needs to understand that the wreckage and wounds of his addiction will take time and effort to heal. But how long does a man have to live in a relationship, practically begging his partner to open up to him emotionally? At what point is the man in recovery not responsible for the pain that his partner continues to live in without doing anything to contribute to healthy change?

This is a very sensitive topic, and I have seen men's consistent love and service to their partners create the space for healing. I have also watched those same men learn how to ask for what they need, set clear boundaries, and learn how to lovingly point out to their partner where his or her behavior is not okay. Through the process of recovery, men who were once emotionally disengaged and/or volatile in their relationships can become the emotional torchbearers. As Marty said, "I know that I experience love through connection. Just by taking some time to connect emotionally, not even physically." Marty didn't always talk like this. Recovery and working the Twelve Steps have given him permission to accept this about himself, regardless of whether it is "manly" or not.

Women are not the only ones who can find themselves in relationships begging for more intimacy and connection and not able to get it from their partner. If you find yourself in this situation, it could become very frustrating and you may find yourself having to make some really difficult decisions. Before you get to that point, do a thorough inventory and talk in depth to your sponsor, closest friends and advisors, and (if you have one) your therapist to examine your behaviors and your reactions to your partner's behaviors. How do you respond to your partner when he or she is shut down or disconnected? How does it serve him or her and the relationship? What is your part? I have worked with a lot of men who found themselves in a cycle where they felt shut off from their partners so they began to look only for the evidence of when their partners were being emotionally distant or disconnected. This is the time when it is extremely important to focus on not just your behavior, but also on how you communicate both verbally and nonverbally, and how accurately you see any efforts your partner might be making. This is a time when making a genuine and collaborative effort to engage in couples counseling can make all the difference. Sometimes the aggrieved partner simply needs the help of someone other than you to see her part in the problems that persist in the relationship. And if he or she also has unresolved trauma from his or her past, it is all the more important for both parties to get individual as well as couples support because when the unresolved traumas of two people collide, the results can be quite explosive.

There are no easy answers in this area, but I cannot stress enough the value of a good couples counselor before making any final decisions. If you find yourself in this position, don't believe the BS out there that says it is automatically the man's fault. Believe that you have a right to have an emotionally available partner. Again, if you are healing from the effects of the addiction, then you may need to have two or three years of quality recovery before you can expect your partner to rejoin you in the partnership. She or he may need to have more evidence in order to have faith that your recovery is real. Rest assured, however, that you do not need to be held hostage by your partner for your past. Once you have sincerely made amends, taken responsibility for your behavior, and begun to change your behavior, your penance is done. Either your partner begins to make an effort to heal and trust again or you get to make the choice as to what is best for you and your recovery.

Into Action

► Think of a past relationship you were in. Look at it from the perspective of both formulas ($\frac{1}{2} + \frac{1}{2} = 1$ and $1 + 1 = 3$). On one side of the paper at the top write the first formula; on the second side of paper at the top write the second formula. For each formula write about how your past relationship met those criteria.

► Imagine you are in your ideal relationship. What would a "complete" partner look like to you? Write it out with as much detail as possible.

► Think about your current (or a past) relationship and times where you wanted to run. What was happening in the relationship at that time? What were some of the ways that you "ran" away from your partner emotionally? Spiritually? Physically?

CHAPTER SEVEN

No Man Is an Island: Men and Asking for Help

"Asking for help or guidance goes against the concept of self-reliance and masculinity." –Bobby

If there is one thing that makes or breaks a relationship and determines whether or not it grows, it would be how we engage support in our lives. What does it mean for a man to ask for help? Not just once, but over and over again, as often as necessary? In keeping with the Man Rules, it comes down to three pernicious words: *not a man*. I may ask for help, but likely not feel great about it. Sure, our society pays lip service to how important it is for a man to ask for help, but when the rubber hits the road, to what extent do we really incorporate support into our lives?

There is something incredibly powerful about men seeking support, because it violates the Man Rules. We are raised to be independent, in charge, right, and confident, and deep inside so many of us is a belief that if we are not, we are weak and we are not real men. As a result, we are disconnected from much of our internal experience. We stay on the surface of things with our small talk, our cleverness, our humor, and our deep knowledge of all things mundane. We put on a front that belies our insecurity and fear.

How do you feel when you ask for help? I don't like it. Despite the numerous times I have done it and the numerous resources I have used throughout my life, I still do not like it. I especially do not like it when asking for help seems to imply that the person I'm asking knows more than I do or that I am wrong or am not competent. Of course, I am wrong all the time and there are myriad things I cannot do. It is not really about that. It is an emotional response and is connected to the shame I still carry about looking or feeling weak or unmanly. Like the vast majority of men, I have a certain block when it comes to seeking support, and a default mode that basically says, "Be a man and fix it yourself. Little boys need help. Real men . . . blah, blah, blah."

This chapter focuses on men's complex relationship with getting support—the push and pull of it. Our relationships fail if we do not get support from others—period. They may not end abruptly; they may just wither on the vine and die a slow death due to emotional distance and lack of communication or conflict resolution.

Women are encouraged to get support from one another and talk about meaningful things. It is the opposite for men. Even those of us who get into recovery and therapy and adjust to the idea of having some kind of support in our lives still often find ourselves going back to the default of "I have to handle this on my own" in its many manifestations.

Think of all of the sources of potential support available in our relationships. Then think about how often you access that support. Think about what gets in the way of accessing it. Despite the fact that I have been living an examined life for many years and have acclimated myself to the idea of mutual support, as I stated above, I still really don't like asking for or getting support. Giving support? Sure. I'll support any man or woman. I love to have the answers and be the expert. I'll admire the hell out of a man for reaching out and showing the humility it takes to ask for help. It *may* even lead me to seek support myself. But making that a regular practice in my life has proven to be quite challenging.

Our Partners

For those of us who are engaged in any long-term, committed relationship, our partner is a very important source of support. Who supports you more than your spouse? Who reaches into parts of you that you didn't even know existed? Who pisses you off as much as they inspire you to be the best man you can be? Who loves you for all that you cannot see and accepts you for all you see too well?

Regardless of our sexual identity and orientation, our partner is our trusted companion. Mark said his relationship with his spouse is "the hardest relationship in my life, and also the most rewarding." Once we make a commitment to another human being, we both basically pull out our maps and say, "Okay, we might have two different maps, but we are in this together." There are times when you go off by yourself and she (or he) goes off by herself, but the commitment is that you always meet back with each other. This is a big part of the "3" in the "1 + 1 = 3" formula from earlier in the book. There is perhaps no other relationship where we try more to find a healthy balance of dependence, independence, and interdependence (explored in more detail in Chapter Twelve, Codependency). When I see my partner as a source of support and someone who can help me, I can be much more honest with her. That takes risk, vulnerability, and trust.

Sharing a common language like the Twelve Steps can be a great benefit to couples seeking to provide mutual support. A majority of the men interviewed identified working the Twelve Steps as a core part of the success of their relationship. Mike said, "I met my wife after I got sober. Through her years in Al-Anon and mine in AA we realized we can get through challenging times and still be okay as individuals and as a couple." Marty said that he needed to focus on "taking care of my side of the street, not hers." The danger lies in using the idea of keeping one's side of the street clean as a way to excuse the continual cleanup of inappropriate, disrespectful behaviors that continue to happen again and again, with little effective change.

I tell my partner, and myself, how I view her by the degree to which I am truly invested in the strength and depth of our connection or being "all in." There are numerous examples of being "all in" that the men I interviewed provided, but two stand out: (1) when you take off the armor enough to share some of the pain you still deal with on a regular basis—for example, when you talk with your partner about abuse you experienced as a child and, without joking about it or making light of it, let him (or her) know how much it hurt you, and perhaps still haunts you; (2) when you find the courage and ability to cry in the presence of your partner *and* allow yourself to be comforted by her (or him). For most of us that is a sacred line, and if we can get there with our partners, there is no going back. What does that mean? For many of us, our greatest pain and vulnerability lie in all of the tears we have stuffed. Sharing that pain in such a naked way and making ourselves so vulnerable provides a special form of freedom. It is also one of the most healing places a man can get to with his partner. Getting to both of those places with Nancy has enabled me to trust her for support more than ever before and created a completely different relationship. It has enabled her to be able to do the same. Both partners need to be willing to do their own work—whatever that looks like for them.

Sponsor/Mentor

Every man (and woman) can benefit from having a sponsor or mentor. In twelve-step culture, sponsorship is very important in supporting a person in his or her recovery. But who doesn't need a trusted advisor they can turn to in times of trouble and confusion, an objective party who cares about us enough to tell us the truth as they see it? As much as human beings want to connect with others and be real with each other, it terrifies us. A sponsor or mentor is a key resource to help bridge that gap between the desire for authentic connection and the fear it evokes.

When we first get into recovery, we have no idea what we are doing—it is a new language, a new philosophy, and a new culture. Jose said, "My sponsor has been a guide through many ups and downs and took me through the life-changing process of the steps." The Twelve Steps seem fairly easy to understand, at least on the surface. A lot of men love checklists, and we view the steps as just that. Of course, we learn the longer we are in recovery that every step is a bottomless well from which we can draw water, and our understanding is constantly evolving and expanding. It is a journey of continuously deepening inquiry, at least if we want it to be. That being the case, we need a solid escort along the way.

Few relationships carry more weight in the twelve-step recovery community than that with a sponsor. If it were not for the four sponsors I have had over the course of my recovery, I would not still be sober and would be far from the man I am today. With their assistance and support, I have discovered who I am in the community of men. I have met very few men in recovery for whom that is not the case. Sponsors help teach men intimacy and how to have relationships.

Many men come into recovery as "fatherless" children. We have had strained or absent relationships with our fathers and we are looking for guidance. Gay or straight, many of us come into the rooms of recovery with a legacy of absent fathering. We are hungry for a father figure, and for many of us our sponsor fulfills that role. Josh said, "I learned how to have a relationship with my dad by building one with my sponsor." This is a very common and important role that the men in recovery play for the men newly sober. Okwas talked about his sponsor in the way a lot of us have experienced our sponsors: "At four years' sobriety I finally found a sponsor I could trust. We went through the Twelve Steps a few times before he died with twenty-seven years of recovery. He helped me find out more about who I am, and later in our recovery he started to fill that father-figure role I needed to help me grow spiritually." Like Josh, Okwas found a man he could trust and then a man who could help him to heal from some of the pain created by the wounds caused by everything his father was unable to give. Even the men who have had close relationships with their fathers have almost never shared the kind of closeness and intimacy that they find in working with a sponsor.

A lot of men, particularly in early recovery, come in with a pretty warped self-perception. As a result of our addiction and past traumas, we are unable to see ourselves, both the best and worst parts of us, clearly. Despite how arrogant some men in early recovery may come off, it is almost always just a cover for how afraid, insecure, and lost they feel. One of the most powerful roles of the sponsor for men in recovery is that of the "mirror." We rely on the mirror to help us see ourselves. A lot of us left childhood with broken mirrors; our perception was distorted and we didn't know it. The question for you is, what do you see in the reflection of your mirror? Exactly who is looking back at you? Sponsors help us answer that question.

Bobby said his sponsor is "authentically, unconditionally supportive of my living in alignment with my own core values." That means he gets what he needs from the mirror, including love, support, responsibility, intimacy, and discipline. We need a sponsor to reflect back the positive changes we've made and the inherent strengths we possess as much as any of our challenges and shortcomings. Nate, an accomplished psychiatrist, described the role his sponsor plays at this point of his recovery (almost thirty years): "My sponsor is a role model and an example of how to live a sober life. He challenges me, yet is very warm and accepting. I can be open and 'tell on myself' when I am around him." A core purpose of the mirror is to build trust and connection in the relationship to foster self-esteem in the individual. Over and over again the men mentioned the theme of trust in their relationship with their sponsor.

Just like in any significant and intimate relationship, the issue of how conflict is handled in a sponsor–sponsee relationship is important. It may start with your sponsor telling you, "Take the cotton out of your ears and put it in your mouth," or "Your best thinking got you here." That is one of the less sophisticated and relational ways that newcomers are informed that they can benefit from talking less, listening more, and evaluating their ideas and reactions in their relationships. At some point a sponsee has to find his own voice in recovery. Even if you have a good sponsor and a close relationship, it is common to have some resentments toward him at some point. When a man is able to talk to his sponsor about these resentments, concerns, and fears that can get in the way of their relationship, it is a positive sign of the evolution of that relationship. Every sponsor should encourage this dialogue knowing they will benefit as much as the man with whom they are working.

So how does a man know what he needs in a sponsor? If we don't have an accurate self-perception, how can we evaluate our needs objectively? It is easy to say, "Find someone who has what you want." But what does that really mean? Here are some things to keep in mind when looking for a sponsor or mentor:

- Don't just listen to what he says in meetings—that can be deceiving.
- Don't just look at what he drives—it could be a rental.

- Don't worry about the man's sexual identity—if he is a healthy man, that is almost irrelevant. If you are a gay man and feel more comfortable at first with a gay sponsor or even a female sponsor, of course, get what you need most to feel safe and to build trust.
- Do talk to other men that he sponsors.
- Don't look for a friend, look for a guide, particularly one who can take you through the steps.
- Do ask yourself and trusted people in recovery (counselor, peers, wise elders) what you think you need from a sponsor so you know.
- Do make your own list of what you would like to have in a sponsor.
- Do talk to a man about how he sponsors, what he expects from you, and what you can expect from him. If he has a problem with any of these questions, you probably just got your answer as to whether he is a good fit for you.

There is a line that is easy to cross for sponsors. That line I'm referring to is the one between a peer in recovery and a professional with specialized training. The boundaries of that role are not always clear. While some men obsess about "outside issues" getting in the way of "pure" sponsorship, there is no question that men need support in all areas of our lives. The challenge for sponsors is in knowing when to support their sponsee in seeking outside help and when to encourage a deeper exploration of the steps. While I truly believe there is nothing that the steps can't help with, I also know that sometimes the steps alone are not sufficient.

Why is that important? Because twelve-step programs have individuals with no professional training at times attempting to direct, cajole, and even coerce men away from support and services that can help them. When a major percentage of the twelve-step community has experienced serious trauma, and for a majority of those their trauma is undiagnosed and untreated, then you have the potential for some serious problems, especially in relationships.

There are amazing men in the recovery community who want nothing other than to pass on the recovery they have been freely given. These men have been freed from the incredible misery of active addiction and want nothing more than to help free others. At their best, the men who sponsor other men in the twelve-step programs are true relational alchemists when they partner with a Higher Power and the recovery community. The alchemy proves as valuable for them as it is for the men with whom they work.

Internal Support

Turning to ourselves and the inner resources we have cultivated is essential to creating a grounded and healthy masculinity. But it is sometimes tricky because we have to face ourselves and all of the junk that exists between our ears. At a certain point we come to realize that perhaps the greatest enemy lies within.

Our relationship with self tends to be rocky, and often even abusive. As Randy said, "If I treated anyone the way I used to treat myself, I would have been arrested. It was not until I began to stop abusing myself and constantly putting myself down that I was truly free to love another." Maybe you've felt as though you're just not cut out to be in an intimate relationship and it is your destiny to live alone or move from conquest to conquest. Or maybe you live in fear of intimacy and have made a long-term commitment to your computer and Internet porn sites. Maybe you believe the myth that men are inherently selfish. Whatever your beliefs about yourself, you will suffer greatly until you become aware of them, make peace with yourself, and choose what beliefs you want to hold about who you are.

One of the greatest internal sources of support and avenues for making peace with ourselves comes through the practice of solitude. Men who cannot practice and become comfortable with some degree of solitude will likely experience relationships that are limited in the capacity for growth and intimacy. Why? Because, as is the case for women, if you use your relationships to help you avoid *you,* then you will forever be looking for someone to fix you, make you happy, and/or take care of you. As a result, you give your power away without even noticing it. Luke said, "I constantly need to connect with my inner self and my Higher Power to recharge and help prevent codependent relationships."

When we slow down, are quiet, and go within ourselves, life unfolds. Rod said, "With solitude comes the deepest of life lessons." How many men do you know who talk about the fear of abandonment? Well, one of the most helpful pieces of wisdom I have received is this: "You can never be abandoned (as an adult) without first abandoning yourself." It is in the experience of solitude that we learn how to *be* with ourselves. We find that we are able to be a very important piece of our own "support puzzle." We begin to recognize when we are abandoning ourselves and how to do something different. Sometimes this is simply sitting with the discomfort, and other times it is connecting with someone else. When we slow down, are quiet, and go within ourselves, life unfolds.

Solitude also teaches us the difference between loneliness and aloneness. Briefly summarized, loneliness comes out of an inability to be comfortable with oneself and in one's own skin; aloneness is the ability to be alone, enjoy one's own company, and still feel connected. You've heard of the "man cave"? When the man cave is used in a healthy way, then that is aloneness. It is men's natural and normal need to have alone time. That is where we find solitude. If we are not careful, we can isolate and use it as an excuse to disconnect from others. But when we experience it in a healthy way, solitude rejuvenates us. It helps us to claim and embrace our independence. Nick said, "It allows me to recharge and collect my thoughts so I can be present in my relationships with others."

Meditation

The regular practice of meditation is important to develop skills around solitude and learning how to simply *be* with oneself. Meditation is indispensable for one's recovery and general peace of mind. It should not be surprising that men are not inherently attracted to something that focuses on being quiet and still—it's not in our DNA, let alone the Rules. Men are "do-ers," not "be-ers." Meditation is our opportunity to listen to God and to life all around us and inside us. It disciplines our mind. It helps to slow down the whirling dervish living in our head. It is very difficult—actually, I would say impossible—to establish any foundation of emotional recovery without some kind of meditation practice.

I have heard many men argue for their meditation to be some kind of activity: fishing, hunting, working out, running, golf, and so on. It is not that these activities cannot be forms of meditation, but there is something very powerful when a man exercises silence and sits still. It goes against our visions of masculinity, which is why so many men resist it. There is nothing wrong with practicing whatever works best for you, but I do really encourage you to try a classic model of meditation. There are many excellent resources to help you learn more about developing a meditation practice. As I heard when I first started actively practicing meditation, "Don't just do something, sit there!"

Higher Power

Jose said, "God is the common denominator with everything that exists in the world around me. When I'm connected I get glimpses of God's grace through people, through nature, and through me." There is perhaps no relationship more baffling and more important than our relationship with a Higher Power (a power greater than us), whether we call it God or something else. This relationship is also a vital source of support for many people. When we seek support from our Higher Power or ask our Higher Power for help, it requires faith, which in turn requires vulnerability and risk. Like my other intimate relationships, the relationship I have with God vacillates. There is a constant dance of connection and disconnection. That is what has made it real for me. The relationship with a Higher Power is very personal. It is for each man to discover and define for himself. Of course, someone can choose to not to have such a relationship and forgo the potential support it can provide.

Like every other important relationship, my relationship with my Higher Power requires me to be as open and honest as I can be. I learned early in my recovery to bring everything to my Higher Power. There is no holding back. It can be a scary thing for someone to tell God to "f$@# off" or to say "I hate you" to God. How can you say such a thing to God? Given all of the times that life has seemed so unfair and all of the times you felt like God let you down, abandoned you, or favored others over you, *how can you not?*

We cannot have a meaningful relationship without any conflict. It works this way with God just as it does with everyone else. How can we truly feel connected or trust them if we are not open about the conflict we feel? What happens when we pretend we are not mad at our best friend or our partner? We are much less likely to seek support or trust that we can be helped—and we will likely slide back into self-reliance and isolation, especially emotional isolation. We can give those feelings to God, all of them—the anger, loneliness, desperation, confusion, doubt (even in God's existence), and everything else. If God is anything like we suspect "it" is, it can handle anything we can give it.

Many men in recovery adopt a belief in a Higher Power because they are told they have to, but they don't clean up the incredible pain from their past relationship with whatever concept of a Higher Power or God they grew up with. For those of us who have suffered trauma, the relationship with God is often compromised. "What did I do to deserve this?" "Where was God when all of this was happening?" "Why didn't God answer my prayers or make it stop?" Those are painful questions that ultimately have no answer. Many men are survivors of spiritual abuse, such as abuse by clergy, abusive religious environments, and parents who used religion to control, demean, and abuse. For these men it can be particularly difficult to heal a relationship with a Higher Power that may have been the source of such pain, abuse, and trauma.

Ultimately, our life philosophy defines us and how we show up in this world. There are many out there for men to choose from, including:

1. The one with the most toys wins.
2. Kill or be killed.
3. Never let them see you sweat.
4. Win at all costs.
5. You're only someone if they know your name.
6. You're on your own.

All of these philosophies are legacies of the Rules. They come out of our pain, our disconnection, and what we think will bring us happiness.

Not one of them fosters or honors relationships. A challenge for me is identifying which of those philosophies influence my behavior. For instance, a part of me still desperately wants to "see my name in lights." Does that drive me anymore? No, but it is there, and either I notice it or it controls me from the shadows. A big part of me wants to destroy those who I perceive have hurt, attacked, or dismissed me or my family. What happens if I act on that? How does that fit with the man I want to be?

Ray talked about how his ideas of being a man have changed with his evolving idea of God: "It has given me an understanding that making mistakes is an important part of the process and that it is through our mistakes and struggles that we experience growth and a desire to improve."

Prayer

Prayer is another way that we can seek support and ask for help primarily in the context of our relationship with our Higher Power or the universe. Prayer is about letting go and being one small part of a very big and ineffable world. Nate said, "It is okay to pray and ask for help. I can turn my will and life over and accept my powerlessness." At least three of the biggest Man Rules are refuted in that statement: Men don't ask for help; men have to be powerful; and men have all the answers. Practicing prayer and treating it as something that builds connection and not just a 911 call moves us more and more out of the bondage of self and into our relationships and a place of humility.

Counseling/Therapy

For a man to enter counseling/therapy is a big deal. There are many reasons for this, but three of the biggest are these: (1) It is the ultimate recognition that he needs help and cannot solve it himself, which may connect to his sense of being a man; (2) there is an inherent vulnerability in going to a therapist that can trigger men's shame and fear; and (3) rightly or wrongly, therapy has been feminized and is often seen as the domain of women, and many men resist it simply for that reason.

In the twelve-step community, choosing to see a counselor/therapist is unfortunately sometimes viewed as failure or a lack of willingness to truly work a program of recovery. It is not difficult to see why many men are hesitant to seek professional support for serious trauma and relationship challenges, even long into their recovery. This is the case even though, as previously stated, the Big Book of Alcoholics Anonymous makes clear that it is important and necessary to take certain problems to outside professionals: "God has abundantly supplied this world with fine doctors, psychologists, and practitioners of various kinds. Do not hesitate to take your health problems to such persons. . . . Try to remember that, though God has wrought miracles among us, we should never belittle a good doctor or psychiatrist."

However, there are many professionals who have little real understanding of addiction or trauma, and who think that medication is the answer for everything. Men in the recovery community are right to be wary of *some* professionals. It is important to find a counselor or therapist who understands addiction and (if trauma is an issue for you) trauma treatment. Ask questions and interview prospective therapists. You get to decide who the best fit is for you. If your sponsor or anyone else is not supportive, if the only thing they can say is a version of "you just need to work the steps more," I would seek counsel elsewhere. Make sure you are truly heard before you decide what you truly need. Don't let someone else's biases prevent you from getting the help you need to give you added peace and happiness in your life and relationships.

Couples Counseling

There is no question that true partnership is very difficult, again more so for men with histories of trauma, because much of our buried pain is unearthed by the vulnerability and intimacy required by those relationships. The closer we get to others, the scarier it is for us. No matter where we are when we get into our relationship, if our relationship is going to survive we have to cross the chasm of intimacy with our partners, which may mean facing some really painful parts of the relationship. For some of the men I interviewed this meant acknowledging infidelity, getting therapy for their anger, dealing with the effects of abuse in the relationship, and even being separated at points. There may be a time when getting outside support in the form of couples counseling will be very helpful.

For couples who want to have fulfilling and intimate partnerships, the potential need for counseling should be expected, rather than viewed as an alarm bell announcing that the relationship is in grave danger. You should know that couples counseling will not work if either person is too disengaged or enmeshed in their partner. For a couples session to be successful, two reasonably invested and individuated people need to enter into it and be able to connect with the therapist. If the therapist is not a good fit for either of you, then find another. Interview therapists together with your partner to get a sense of what works for you as a couple. It took Nancy and me several tries before finding the right therapist, and she has been a vital resource for us. A good couples counselor functions as a coach who has equal affinity for both partners and does not take sides or show favoritism. **Note:** *If there is abuse in the relationship, the dynamic will need to be different. Until safety can be secured, there will be an imbalance in the support the counselor offers (leaning toward the person who is experiencing the abuse), and that should always be the case.*

Contrary to popular belief, sometimes men are the ones who want the support and they find their partner unwilling, for various reasons, to engage in it. Get the support you need. Do a very thorough inventory and talk in depth to your sponsor, closest friends and advisors, and (if you have one) your therapist to get feedback on your behaviors and your reactions to your partner's behaviors. How do you respond to them when they are shut down or disconnected? I have known some men who found themselves in a cycle where they constantly felt shut off from their partners, so they began to look only for evidence of their partner being emotionally distant or disconnected. This is a time when making a genuine and collaborative effort to engage in couples counseling can make all the difference in the world. Sometimes the aggrieved partner simply needs someone other than you to help them see their part in the problems that persist in the relationship.

Men have as much right to have an emotionally available partner as women. If you are new(er) to recovery and you and your partner are still healing from the effects of active addiction, it is helpful to know that you may need to have two or three years of quality recovery before you can expect your partner to rejoin you in the partnership. She (or he) needs to have faith that your recovery is real. Nonetheless, rest assured you do not need to be held hostage by your partner for your past, including any of the harms you may have caused. Once you have sincerely made amends, taken responsibility for your behavior, and begun to change it, your penance is done. Either your partner makes an effort to heal and trust again or you get to make the choice that is best for you and your recovery.

Meetings

Mutual support meetings are a training ground for relationships. They are the place where our experience developing healthier relationships often begins. Addiction and addictive behaviors deeply affect our relationships, poisoning all of them. Meetings are where we get rejuvenated and fill up our fuel tanks to continue on the journey toward creating and maintaining healthy relationships. If you went to treatment, you may have started to test the waters with relationships and perhaps met some people you have been and will stay connected to. But meetings are out in the world, in your community, wherever you live, and, unlike treatment, which is very temporary, twelve-step meetings and other mutual support groups will always be an available support resource.

Men's Meetings

About men's meetings, Jim, who is a gay man, stated, "I often think I am missing some big, secret part to being a man, some knowledge that was given to all men but me at some point in their development. Men's meetings help dispel that belief." I was in recovery for eleven or twelve years before I made a men's meeting a regular part of my program. I encourage you not to wait that long. When I interviewed the men for this book, almost every single one of them spoke about the fear they had of other men before recovery. This fear came out in many different ways. Often it showed up as separation and a constant sense of competition and even adversarial posturing. The men were afraid that other men would make fun of them or reject them if they shared what was really happening in their lives. But unlike in other settings, that rarely happens in the rooms of recovery. For some, the men they encounter at meetings might be their first role models in the process of learning how to be a healthy man.

I am learning how to be a man thanks to these meetings, by watching these other men as they share their authentic struggles and successes. According to the Rules, it's such an "unmanly" thing to do. We want to find and begin to model ourselves after the men who "have what we want" in terms of character, comportment, and spirituality. We see these men, listen to their stories of where they came from compared to where they are now, and think to ourselves, *If they could do it, maybe I can, too.* It's important to be aware that all men's meetings are different, and some are much healthier than others. There are some men's meetings that are the equivalent of good ol' boys' clubs. What does that mean? Some gatherings of men play into the stereotypes and reinforce the unhealthy behaviors that emanate from the Man Rules. It is essential to seek out the meetings that have what you need for your own recovery process.

Meetings are there, first and foremost, for those of us who are actively suffering. We need a safe place to bring our pain in a society that still does not understand addiction or the recovery process. In truth, all meetings are people coming together trying to be as honest and vulnerable as they are capable of being about what is truly happening in their lives. Who couldn't benefit from having such a supportive resource in their life? In meetings we are reminded that we are no better and no worse than anyone else, and that we need to continue to learn and grow. Meetings are there to help us move increasingly into intimacy and vulnerability and, in turn, authenticity.

There is nothing greater than success, be it material or spiritual, to fool a man into believing that he no longer needs the support system that helped him achieve that success. At the heart of it are (you guessed it) the Rules. I have yet to meet a man—regardless of the amount of time he has been in recovery—who doesn't want to be able to do *it* on his own in some way. The resistance to continuing, as necessary, to ask for, accept, and offer help is the greatest impediment to achieving and maintaining long-term recovery.

Men's Work

There is something powerful about going beyond the confines of a recovery meeting and going deep with other men in the journey of healing. It is particularly powerful for men to be able to truly see the trauma that operates in our lives and to allow ourselves to be seen a little more authentically than we may feel comfortable or safe doing in mutual support meetings. Earl said, "My life is sourced in men's work. It's in those groups that I find the most intimate groups of people I have in my life. I feel I give myself the most expansive range of emotional risk, and am most helped to be the strong and accountable man I want to be in those circles. Because of being anchored in my men's groups, I can take the needed risks in my marriage and other life relationships. It's given me the capacity to intuitively solve problems that used to baffle me."

It is one thing for me to preach the importance of men dealing with their trauma and creating deeper and more intimate relationships with other men, and it is another thing to do it. It is hard. It is messy. It is painful. It requires great vulnerability. And it is beautiful. I had been training on and speaking about male trauma for almost three years when I did the first men's retreat I had done in over a decade. Stuff was being stirred up for me all the time. This was a group of men, all of whom are professionals in the addiction field, committing to come together once a year to do their personal work. I had been longing for a group like this.

I can look at so much of what happened at that first retreat in the context of the work I do and the focus of this book. I had been yearning to do some deeper work because I knew that it would help me be more effective in all of my relationships, notably my relationship with my wife and my daughter, who at the time was only two years old. The work at that retreat was a true blessing that opened up a very intense year of doing personal trauma work, including a weeklong intensive retreat, EMDR, and some targeted therapy.

I entered the second retreat with a new foundation of skills and resources for taking care of myself as a result of the intense work I had done over the course of that year, much of it focused on trauma. All of the men come to the retreat with the expectation of "doing work." While you are not forced to do anything, and the work can look any way it needs to and can take the form that helps you feel safest—you are coming to do work.

I knew I needed to go somewhere I had never gone in all of my years of doing men's work and all of the different men's meetings and retreats. It was time for me once and for all to be seen by these men and share with them the pain and anguish I still carried, even after almost a quarter of a century, around my growth problem during adolescence and all of the trauma connected to it. I got up and just started talking. It all came out. These men were amazing. They supported me and loved me. I felt raw and exposed, and yet I also felt very safe. I felt like they had seen me in a way that I had rarely ever allowed. Many of the men thanked me. I was more real with those men than I had been in a long time, in some ways ever. It opened up a deeper conversation with Nancy when I came home. It opened up the trauma work I had been doing over the previous year, all the way to the point where I am right now as I write this book. Finally, for the first time in my life, I shared from the depths of my pain and anguish the constant conversation that had been tearing me apart, telling me I'm not a man. Instead of separating me from the other men as a result of that incredible vulnerability and rawness, I let that bring me closer to them. I leaned into it.

There are two incredibly important variables that have made the retreats I spoke about above such successes: male facilitators who have done their own work and an environment that provided the highest degree of emotional safety. These are essential. Can women facilitate men's work? Sure. Are men going to hold back some of their truths because women are facilitating? Very possibly. However, what is most important is that men learn that we can do this very deep and vulnerable work with other men.

The importance of emotional safety cannot be overstated. The male facilitators who led both of my most recent retreats worked very hard to create a safe place for all of us, and constantly checked in with us to see how we were doing. They also helped us to share in the responsibility of maintaining that safety for ourselves and others. They made it clear that we could work as deeply as we wanted. If that merely meant acknowledging in front of the group that you knew you had some work to do, that was awesome, and as respected as anyone else's work.

Men's retreats come in all shapes and sizes. There are recovery-focused retreats. There are also retreats that are explicitly spiritual in nature, ranging from Christian to more open, nondenominational forms of spirituality. A lot of men's retreats are based upon Jungian philosophy and models developed in the seventies and eighties that discuss four different male archetypes: the warrior (accountability and integrity in relationships), the lover (connected and relational), the magician (creative and spiritual), and the king (leader and decision-maker). The term used for some of those retreats is *mythopoetic,* influenced strongly by the poetry and work of people like Robert Bly, who wrote *Iron John,* one of the few books to break through the supposed "men don't buy books about personal growth" barriers.

There is a men's retreat for you. Find one; research it; ask good questions of the organizers, facilitators, or other men you know who have gone on them; and GO! These retreats are for all men—not just men in recovery. It allows us to see that we all have wounds and that we can truly be seen by one another and be the better for it. My hope is that a time will come when these retreats are considered the norm for how men support themselves, and, for men in recovery, that they happen in a man's first or second year of recovery. Of course, it is also my hope that men will talk openly about their trauma in their recovery meetings to help facilitate this awakening even more.

There is something sacred about the places where we can show up as more real than we have ever been able to before. That is a gift, and one that those who love us will experience the benefits of as much as anyone. Ray talked about his experiences doing men's work and the relationships he has been able to forge as a result when he said, "I have great friends who inspire me to be a better man as I strive to do the same for them."

Into Action

► Identify your sources of support.
  • Identify whom you can trust enough to ask for help
    when you need it.
  • What do you need to do to develop and enlarge your
    support system?

► Think about a recent situation in which you didn't ask for
  help when you knew you could have benefited from some.
  What kept you from reaching out? What were the Man
  Rules that got in the way?

► Think about a situation in which you recently asked for help.
  How did you feel before you reached out? What Man Rules
  were getting in the way? What Man Rules helped you?
  How did you feel after?

► Identify five things you need help or support with. Write
  about what has kept you from getting that support. Identify
  who you can get support from and reach out to them, then
  write in your notebook what it was like to get that support.
  It may help you if you share this with someone else to help
  you to take action.

I cannot overstate how much I encourage you to find a group
of men. Don't settle. Don't sell yourself short. Fight for your
best self. Find the best men to lead you to being the best man
you can be. What you need is out there.

CHAPTER EIGHT
Shame and Vulnerability

"Shame makes me feel flawed and unworthy of love and acceptance. I have felt that I deserve to be mistreated. It becomes a vicious cycle. When I feel shame, I can act in a manner that fosters more shame." –Nate

Have you ever been embarrassed to ask for directions because you didn't want to look stupid or incompetent as a man? A lot of us have. That voice that berates us is shame. It is the voice that, when we listen to it, prevents us from seeing our landscape accurately in the moment, has us taking all kinds of wrong turns, and ultimately gets us lost. It then keeps us from admitting we are lost!

The best definition of shame I have heard is this: Shame says you didn't make a mistake; rather, *you are* a mistake. When the men I know are gut-wrenchingly honest with themselves, they begin to realize the degree to which shame has impacted their lives. Letting go of shame requires us to acknowledge all of the beliefs that have to do with feeling "less than" or feeling as though we don't belong. Letting go of shame requires us to expose some of our deepest and most fundamental wounds—wounds that are so rooted that they have become part of our psyche. Luke talked about it this way: "I carried shameful and painful secrets about what I did and what happened to me in the past, and I wasn't going to ever tell anyone about them. Revealing those secrets and that shame in recovery has had a powerful impact on my healing."

There are many ways that shame can show up in our lives. There seem to be layers of shame. The first and most obvious one for those of us in recovery is the shame we feel for all of the things we did while active in our addiction. Part of that shame is healed simply by showing up at meetings where others have had similar experiences and, instead of feeling ashamed and beating themselves up, they are laughing. Learning to laugh at ourselves and to see our utter and common humanity is a powerful antidote for shame. We heal a lot of our shame in community.

If I could fault myself for previously overlooking something central to men's experience, it would be shame. I was wading through my own shame even as I was writing my first book. There was the voice inside telling me I was a fraud and had no business writing the book. The voice told me I was a horrible writer and said I didn't deserve to have a published book or success of any kind. All of these negative, judgmental voices that tormented me throughout the process were just part of the life to which I had become so accustomed. They were the filthy germs and dirt that had clouded the Water for me growing up, and I had no idea how much they continued to color how I saw myself and the world.

Part of the truth for me was what Jose described: "It almost felt easier in the past to sit in the shame." For me, as much suffering as it created, it was familiar. At some level I had internalized that I did not deserve to be happy or to feel good about myself. Like Nate, my shame helped to contribute to the idea or belief that I didn't deserve to have a good life. The other part is that I was unaware of the voices of my shame. I could not separate them from who I was. Like a lot of men who have done several Fourth and Fifth Steps (owning my behaviors, being able to see my part in my resentments, getting honest about my fears, diving deep into my confusion about sexuality, and, of course, fully conceding to my innermost self about my addiction), I thought that I had addressed all of my shame. But that was just the shame associated with violating my value system that had grown out of my addiction. But I only began to touch the deep core of the shame that came from my childhood and adolescent experiences after writing *A Man's Way through the Twelve Steps*.

Finally, I took the risk to talk about it all. All of the things torturing me for years I began to share with Nancy and the men with whom I am closest. I no longer am fighting the battle by myself. I admit when I am lost, let others point me in the right direction, and trust them to do so. Are those voices of shame gone? Absolutely not. But they are quieter, and I am less likely to believe them. Or to allow myself to be tortured by them.

Bob talked about wrestling with his shame over twenty-plus years of recovery this way: "Roadblocks are the worst when they are unseen and unnamed. Whenever my shame is unseen and unnamed it controls me, and I move into risky territory, sometimes to slip into addictive states, sometimes to get lucky and not slip." Over the course of my recovery I have experienced many slips into addictive and unhealthy behavior that led me to feel more shameful.

Trauma and shame feed each other. As Larry said compellingly: "Shame is trauma." First, shame is what keeps the pain of trauma alive. Second, trauma also helps to create shame, because when we internalize the ill intentions of others and personalize the tragedies of life, we tend to make up things about ourselves—especially as children, because we do not know any better. These negative beliefs then define a lot of our lives, especially our inner lives. Okwas said, "Learning about the true meaning of shame really helped me walk through each of my traumas." As we begin to let go of shame, we find ourselves more and more able to speak to the truth of our trauma. The more we strive to tell the whole truth of our experience, the more shame begins to fade from our lives.

Healing from our shame requires digging deep into the muck, holding it in our hands, bringing it out into the sunlight by sharing it with others, and watching as the filth falls through our hands. For so many men, a core shame message is: *I am not a man.* This is exactly what Randy said as he thought about his struggles facing shame: "At the beginning, I felt my shame made me less of a man." I've heard many men say the same thing. If I have these feelings or admit to these feelings, I am weak, which makes me less of a man.

One of the men I interviewed said that shame was not a big issue for him, and then later in the interview talked about how challenging it has been, and continues to be, for him to notice and deal with his shame. I think this dissonance typifies a lot of men's relationship to shame. We have some sense it is there but, because so many of us see shame as being about weakness and unmanliness, we tell ourselves that we do not have a lot of shame. That is what I did for a very long time. Only recently have I been able to be aware of when I am experiencing shame and communicate that to the people to whom I am closest.

There is no question that men do *not* like to feel weak. Guy said it perfectly when I asked him how his ideas of being a man kept him from dealing with the shame in his life: "Suck it up, buttercup" was the mantra he got growing up, and then the one he has been shaming himself with ever since. Men do *not* like to feel insecure or afraid, or admit that they have those feelings. Why? Because it goes against the Rules: They are not manly. We are afraid that someone will revoke our putative "man card." The truth is, as Brené Brown discusses in *Men, Women, and Worthiness,* women *do* reject us sometimes for our vulnerability. Women also respond through the lens of the Rules because they internalize and buy into them in the same way as men. And so we hide our shame. We tuck shame-based messages and the experiences that go with them deep inside, and so they rule us. They keep us disconnected in our relationships. Or, said differently, they allow us to connect only so much.

Sean said it perfectly: "Shame is a dungeon that prevents the various parts of ourselves from becoming whole. We have to tear down those walls." I know Sean and I know how incredibly hard he has worked to tear down those walls. The collective experience of the men I've interviewed says it takes time. We didn't build those walls overnight— they have been built, fortified, and rebuilt even stronger and more impenetrable, over decades. They will not fall overnight. And even if they fall, it doesn't mean we won't build new ones. For example, a man might let his spouse know that he is angry. Then maybe the same situation elicits a response where he is not sure what is going on but he doesn't lash out and push his partner away. Then, the next time, he realizes after taking a long, deep, and slow breath that what he is feeling is actually *hurt.* He doesn't share it, but he knows it. Then, maybe, the next time he really takes the risk and shares that he feels hurt. In so doing, he lets the walls down, makes himself vulnerable to attack, and yet feels liberated. That is the progression of slowly releasing the iron grip of shame on our hearts. That was my experience.

The question deep inside so many men is: *Am I man enough?* How do I rectify all of the stuff happening to me internally with who I am supposed to project to the outside world? If so much of my internal life does not jibe with the Man Rules, what does that mean about me and my value as a man?

I talked earlier about the metaphor of The House from the curriculum I codeveloped: The idea is that every man (and woman) has an outside and inside of his or her house (self). As men, we put a lot of our energy into the outside of the house so it looks good—the cars, the clothes, the professional success, the good-looking wife (because "*real* men" are not openly gay), and so on. The only problem is that while we put so much of our attention on the outside, we neglect the inside. In fact, the inside often falls apart as we ignore the signs of disrepair and distress that are too uncomfortable to face. If we are ashamed of what's on the inside, then we won't let anyone get close to us. People keep coming over to our house and saying, "Wow, it looks so good on the outside; how about the inside?" And the more they like us, the more they want to see inside. This is only human. "Let me know you." But what happens when we show them the inside of our house? We can be standing in the entryway and it feels incredibly uncomfortable because the other person is going to see what a mess the inside is. At that point, we have to start seeing it too. As a result, we avoid intimacy and sabotage relationships so that others don't get access to the inside. Often, the other person simply gives up.

We protect our shame and the feelings associated with it by putting a lot of energy into not looking weak. Once we get over the concern about looking weak and finally feel safe enough to let someone in, then she or he gets to experience what is underneath the shame. Underneath men's experience of shame is what seems to be the core of women's as well: not feeling lovable, not being good enough, not deserving to be happy or have peace in one's life. That is what I hear over and over again from men who have done a lot of personal work and feel safe. The truth is, men grow up in a cauldron of shame. In effect, many of us learn the

Man Rules by being shamed into abandoning or denying our authentic selves.

As little boys, shame is one of the most destructive (and effective) tools that people use to put us in our place and make sure that we follow the Rules. Shame becomes the number-one overseer to make sure that men stay within the Rules. Inside of shame is our "weakness," our fear, our insecurity, and our vulnerability. On the other side of shame is an acceptance of our authentic self and the personal power that arises from the experience of embracing and honoring that true self. As I have said throughout this book, only you can really know who you are. We need others to help us on that journey, but at the end of the day you are the one who gets to step into the man you want to be. In all honesty, that truth is still unfolding for me, and I allow myself to be more fully who I am every day. As a result, I feel more like a man than I ever have.

Vulnerability

We cannot heal from shame without stepping into our vulnerability. In fact, I do not think you can have meaningful recovery or relationships if you are not able to step into vulnerability. Which of the Twelve Steps does not come with some element of vulnerability?

If shame is the belief that there is something inherently and fundamentally wrong with you, the way you heal from all of the ways that corrosive thread has woven itself around your life is by taking the risk of facing those lies and sharing them with others. When we allow ourselves to be seen—emotionally and spiritually naked—and we survive it, little by little we erase shame from our lives. That comes through the process of vulnerability.

Vulnerability is trained out of us starting very early in our lives. We are socialized from a very young age that vulnerability is a sign of weakness. Bobby said the greatest challenge for him in dealing with the shame in his life was "overcoming the internalized belief that shame equals weakness." Every man I interviewed talked about the two opposing forces of vulnerability: the struggle to be vulnerable and how much it takes for them to be able to do it, and the power and freedom they experience when they allow themselves to be vulnerable. Larry said that the biggest challenge for him in dealing with shame has been "becoming vulnerable and staying vulnerable." Allowing ourselves to be vulnerable takes incredible courage.

Vulnerability goes directly against the Man Rules. Jim described the paradox of vulnerability: "In order to gain true intimacy, you have to be open to being hurt." Most men do not have a lot of practice in being vulnerable, and so we are not quite prepared for the impact it has on us. David talked about how vulnerability can show up in gay men's relationships: "As a man who loves men, if I'm seen as too vulnerable, then I may seem weak, a quality I was more accepting of when I dated women." Even for gay men, who tend to reject a lot of macho posturing, the internalization of the Rules can have problematic effects on romantic relationships. Vulnerability does not mean you *might* get hurt; it means you *will* get hurt. The question is, how do you respond to it?

Men need to know how to deal with the aftereffects of vulnerability as much as we need to learn how to be vulnerable. Many men have connected with others at very deep levels—sharing their deepest wounds—only to turn on those same people in an effort to protect themselves. How many men have turned their backs on, and even destroyed, the most important and meaningful relationships in their lives because the other person got too close?

If we want to be closer to others, we have to let them inside, behind the walls we have put up to protect ourselves from the possibility of being hurt. Bobby said that vulnerability is all about "trusting others with our human fears and shortcomings." Our ability to own the less-than-attractive parts of us creates intimacy. We all wear different masks at different times. We cannot help but feel vulnerable when we take off one of our masks. This can also be extremely difficult for women to do, but the Rules create special obstacles that usually make it harder for men.

The Anger Funnel + Shame = Rage

During the last years of my active addiction and the first decade of my recovery I spent most of my time angry and enraged, which prevented me from seeing the truth underlying so much of my anger: shame.

Remember the anger funnel I described earlier? When we add toxic shame to the anger funnel, the result is often rage.

We back men into a corner emotionally and tell them the only acceptable feelings are anger or nothing. Then we shame this Rule into men. Add in the emotional, verbal, physical, and sexual abuse that so many men experience, and is it any wonder that so many men are so angry? Does it really surprise us that rage is such a struggle for many men?

There are few spaces that can safely hold men's rage. It scares a lot of us, especially those of us who have been hurt by men's rage. It also scares those of us who have struggled with our own rage and have hurt others, even when we were working to heal from its damaging effects. Rage explodes on others like a flamethrower, burning those who are caught in its path. Rage turned inward becomes deep depression. But when we try to shut down a man who is raging, it's like trying to put out a grease fire with water. It only makes the fire larger.

Sitting with shame is painful because there is nobody to blame. When I truly begin to embrace shame, I have to admit how badly I feel about myself. Bobby talked about his challenges overcoming "a belief that I AM the problem, rather than I am dealing with a problem." Bobby also described his struggles with regard to being angry and abusive toward the people in his life. For a long time he considered himself to be a tough boss with high expectations of his employees when he was actually ruling by intimidation.

One of my favorite quotes from graduate school is: "Silence and secrecy are the shelter for power." That is an excellent description of shame. Shame leaves you feeling powerless and thrives in the darkness of fear, isolation, macho posturing, arrogance, and rage. Of course, before we can heal our shame, we have to admit that it is there.

Nobody else can get rid of shame for you. They can love you. They can tell you how wonderful you are. They can support you in doing the work to free yourself from the chains of shame, but you have to walk through it. And it can feel as if you are peeling away a layer of your own skin. The greatest freedom that comes from facing our shame is that we can be seen for who we are, without the armor, without yet another mask to hide behind. When I first started sharing all of the things about which I felt shame, numerous lies about myself that I had been carrying around for decades came out. The feeling of freedom I experienced was incredible. I slowly began to be more and more accepting of myself. The internal chaos and self-criticism became quieter. And I was double-digit years into my recovery. Mark said the struggle for him has been "feeling weak, broken, and unworthy," and doing the work anyway. It is, as the poet Rumi wrote, a door upon which we have been knocking, not realizing it was locked from the inside.

This is where faith in a Higher Power or something bigger than you comes in. When you have faith that you're going to be okay, you have the ability to walk through the pain, speak your truth even when it scares the hell out of you, and show up in your relationships authentically. Be open and willing to learn from other men and women. Listen to where your Higher Power is leading you and be willing to move in that direction. When you know who you are, all of your other relationships will fall into place, and fall away if need be.

Shame requires us to face everything inside us that we think is not manly. As Rod said, the key for him in dealing with his shame is "not believing the lies." Paradoxically, when we face all of those things we have the chance to become real men. To become the best men we can be, we find the skin that fits us best. When we let go of shame, we can own parts of who we are that we think are going to get us laughed at, rejected, and hurt.

A New Strength

When I told Luke I was writing this book, he sent me a long email imploring me to address the importance of how men connect with other men: "I want you to talk about how hard it is for men to be with one another . . . and how fucked up that is." We learn very quickly as boys that other boys are not in our lives for intimacy, and that continues, for the most part, throughout our adult life. Ricardo talked about being able to be *with* men now: "I am able to care for other men now and feel their pain." In the past Ricardo protected himself with anger and violence and never thought that anyone else would care about his pain, especially not another man. Okwas said, "I can have a normal conversation with men now. I don't need to be on my guard. Letting my walls down has been the hardest part." Two words came up over and over again in my interviews with the men when I asked them about what had changed the most in their relationships with other men: trust and vulnerability.

Are you going to hurt me? That is in the back of every man's head as he slowly steps into trusting another man. Not a lot of men can admit that— to themselves or someone else. Men don't talk about getting hurt or being afraid of being hurt. Nate talked about how this had changed for him: "I do not view other men as rejecting and cold anymore. I am able to see the vulnerable side and to feel acceptance. I used to feel inferior, insecure, and unlikable. I set myself apart from other men. Now I seek out relationships and feel like I have something to contribute."

The other question we ask is: *Am I going to have to hurt you?* When men step into other men's inner lives, it is serious business. Like walking a minefield, we never know when we might accidentally hit a mine that we could not see that sets the whole relationship off. Bobby said that the most important factor in his relationships with other men is "ensuring safety and both men offering mutual vulnerability." What a tall order! How do two people who have not been taught to value or ensure the emotional safety of others do it for themselves and each other?

Too many men jump in too deep and/or too soon and are not prepared for the strength it takes to stay afloat in the waters of intimacy and vulnerability. Okwas said, "I would consider my strength as being able to trust and be trusted by the men I have allowed into my life through meetings." That did not happen overnight for me, Okwas, or for any of the men I interviewed. We only build trust slowly, and once that happens you increase the likelihood that you will get hurt, be let down, and have other very human and painful experiences that occur in relationships. You also increase the likelihood of experiencing a connection with another man that you may have never thought possible.

Trust means that you are willing to walk through the conflict and not just cast the relationship aside when you encounter the inevitable problems. What is it like to honor our weaknesses with other men? What's it like to hold another man's most painful moments and experiences in our hands with care and love? Nick described this beautifully: "I love sports, sex, and power, and I am also very capable of being deeply emotionally intimate and listening to men's souls while holding mine in check or sharing deeply myself." That is the description of a healthy and balanced man.

Embracing Shame

Any man who wants to be successful in his relationships has to get to a place where he is able to embrace shame. Remember the phrase from earlier—*name it, trace it, face it, and embrace it*? The Twelve Steps work wonderfully on shame in many ways because they provide a structure through which we gather in community and learn how to show up as honestly and openly as we are able. We are constantly risking being vulnerable, sharing a little more of our true selves. Meetings are nothing more than all of us figuring out how to be real with each other. Who can't benefit from that?

How do men embrace shame? Slowly. If we try to rip ourselves out of our shame, we are likely to be too exposed and raw, with the potential for it to have the opposite effect of reinforcing the shame. I cannot say how many clinicians I have worked with who get excited about working with men who have had incredible breakthroughs in making themselves vulnerable and open, only to find them dropping out of services a week or two later. What many do not realize is that when a man has a breakthrough in exposing some very vulnerable part of his life or who he is, at first it is likely to engender more shame rather than less. The man probably needs twice as much support in the days *after* such a revelation as he does in that moment.

When Rick and I conduct trainings, we talk about how important it is to help men walk through their vulnerability. Men seem to have two challenges: to feel safe enough to become vulnerable, and to understand that the impact of the vulnerability may not be felt until hours, or days, or even weeks later. Brené Brown has the perfect term for this: vulnerability hangover. In other words, when we connect with someone at a vulnerable level, we want to prepare ourselves for some intense feelings—including shame and regret—to come up afterward. Those feelings can lead us to pull away and disconnect from others, especially those to whom we are closest, all in the name of attempting to protect ourselves—sometimes at the expense of the relationship. Many men do that with anger, abusiveness, and abandonment—all in the name of trying to keep themselves safe.

With the best of intentions, I hear a lot of people encourage men to step into their vulnerability without helping them understand the possible repercussions of such steps. I had to learn the hard way that vulnerability for men is a very delicate process. I found myself deeply wanting someone to truly know me, yet when I would open up a wound and share it, I felt so raw. Often I was retraumatizing myself with no awareness of it. I would then almost instinctively lash out at the person with whom I had just shared something incredibly intimate. I felt too vulnerable and did not know how to manage the intensity of the feeling.

We also need to be very careful about with whom we are vulnerable. Especially in early recovery, men (or women) frequently try to compensate for years of secretiveness and dishonesty by sharing with anyone and everyone about anything and everything. Yikes! Maintaining good boundaries, safety, and trust are important considerations against which sharing deeply personal information needs to be balanced. But we often need to be taught those skills. We need "vulnerability coaches" who can help us step-by-step through the process, including recognizing the different reactions we may have. As Rick often points out when we are training clinicians, it is important to remember that for some men who are early in the process of healing from their pasts, trust and safety are not interchangeable concepts. A man may initially need to not trust, or to trust only in small increments, in order to feel safe.

"Holy Shit! I Am the Patriarchy . . . "

Author's note: The title from this section comes from Brené Brown when she realized through her research on men and shame how much women are guilty of reinforcing the Man Rules and keeping men stuck in that false persona.

Rick and I were doing a training and were checking in with the group at the beginning of the second day. One gentleman spoke about an exchange with his wife the previous night. It happened to be the night that Mariano Rivera was retiring from the New York Yankees and baseball after an incredible career. That means it was one of the nights that the Rules take the night off and men are freely allowed to get emotional, especially if they have had a few beers. In his farewell speech, Mariano got very emotional and began to cry. The man's wife looked at him and saw that he was also getting emotional and said, "So, what, are you going to cry now?"

And there it was. She verbalized a lot of the judgments that women carry around inside them, often without any awareness. They sometimes don't see the Water any better than we do, especially *our* part of the Water. Many women think they see all of the Water because they sometimes see *their* Water. This man's response was beautiful: "Yeah, well, maybe I am. I am allowed to cry, too!" She didn't know how to respond. I then asked him what the likelihood was that he would have said the same thing a month ago. "No chance. I would have told her to shut up or made fun of Mariano or both." But he didn't, and as a result his wife has the chance to see her husband differently, if she can handle it. He had the opportunity to be more of himself and chose to take advantage of it, and that can transform their relationship.

Women often say how much they want a man who is sensitive, is vulnerable, and shares his feelings. They want a man who is not forceful and doesn't try to control everything. Guess what happens when you give women *that* man? They often don't know what to do with him. That is when they have the chance to see how much of the Man Rules they have taken on. In trainings I joke that women will say, "Holy crap, I wanted you to open up, but not that much." That is what so many men fear from the women in our lives—that we will open the gates of the steel fortress where we have been hiding and we will be attacked. We will be mocked. We will find that we are not safe.

It is not healthy to take off all of the armor that you've worn for perhaps a lifetime and stand there defenseless and exposed. It is important to start slowly and work up to it. You can start by removing your helmet, or exposing your hands. One of the hardest things a man can do is accept himself for who he is and embrace that person, irrespective of previous perceptions of being a man or the Man Rules.

Nate said the biggest challenge for him in dealing with his shame has been "learning to love myself despite my shame." What would it take for you to truly love yourself? It is not nearly as simple as saying, "But I do love myself."

My experience is that the more I can accept myself for who I am—all of me—the less shame controls my life. If I am okay with me, then it doesn't matter so much what you think of me. There is, however, something very powerful and healing about getting acceptance from other human beings, especially those to whom we are the closest. True love is based upon both individuals sharing themselves, warts and all, and loving each other just the same. We are lovable even if someone knows all of us. We can pretend that as long as you love yourself, you don't need anything from anyone to feel okay. But who really gets there? I have found that the power of my most meaningful relationships has really been that we are both invested in learning how to love while being willing to make mistakes in order to get there. The truth of this is no different for men than it is for women. The desire—and the fear—to be known is a profoundly human experience.

Into Action

▶ In your journal, write down three things you used to be ashamed about and three things you still feel shame about.

▶ How did you get over the shame of the three things you used to feel ashamed about?

▶ Would you be willing to choose one of the three things you feel shame about now and share it with one of the people to whom you are closest?

▶ In your journal, write down one thing you have been holding back from sharing in one of your most important relationships and why you have been holding it back.

▶ Choose three relationships.
  • Talk to the people with whom you have those relationships about the ideas in this chapter.
  • Share with them one thing you still struggle with feelings of shame about.
  • Offer them the chance to share something they used to feel shame about or still do, if they feel comfortable doing so.

CHAPTER NINE
Violence and Abuse

"All men were abusive and were to be feared; all women were abusive, therefore deserved to be abused." —Anonymous

"I am very careful to not say or do what was done to me." —Anonymous

"It's hard to look in the mirror most days." —Anonymous

Author's note: In my efforts to be trauma-informed, I want to let you know that this chapter may be triggering for you. Please take care of yourself when you read it. If you experience painful memories or any other kind of discomfort, stop reading and do some self-care. You can use any of the self-care suggestions at the end of Chapter Three. The material in this chapter could trigger you because of your experiences as someone who has survived abuse, but it could also trigger you as someone who has perpetrated abuse and violence. That response is understandable and very healthy. Don't let the shame prevent you from experiencing the pain of memories from when you were far from the man you desire to be. However, also remember the golden rule: **Whatever happened to you as a child was not your fault; AND if you are engaged in any abusive or violent behavior, you are 100 percent responsible and it must stop now.**

If you find yourself being triggered, please also consider seeking some of the support listed in Chapter Seven.

So, take a deep breath. And, as you read, keep breathing.

We cannot talk about men's relationships without including violence and abuse, both experienced and perpetrated. These are the jagged rocks and mountainous areas that we may not be able to see on the map until we get to them. This is not meant to imply that all men are violent or that men are responsible for all violence in relationships. That is not the case at all. But let's be honest: The Man Rules prioritize power and control, and power and control are often exercised though violence. In our society, as well as in many others (and much more so in some), being abusive or violent is almost a part of becoming a man, if only in very subtle ways.

We need to have a much better understanding of what abuse and violence look like. I have found that many men do not have a comprehensive understanding of what they are. In fact, until I started looking at these two concepts, I didn't either. I would still yell or slam doors, thinking that was keeping me from being violent and abusive. Can you identify? What about silence? A lot of men don't realize how we can disconnect and retreat in ways that are unhealthy for our relationships, if not outright abusive.

Violence and abuse significantly tainted my childhood and adolescence, and almost destroyed my recovery and many close relationships. The primary source of my pain as an adult was that I was stuck in a cycle of having my trauma triggered by intense shame, projecting my pain onto other people, and acting out violently and abusively, sometimes without even knowing it, and then going into a shame attack over my behavior. This would happen over and over again. I pushed people away, and the closer they got, the more I pushed them away. It is a huge issue in the recovery community, with much of it due to the trauma that is suffocating so many people. For years into my recovery I found myself hurting the people with whom I was closest and cared most about.

Many men have internalized the abuser(s) they grew up with so that they continue to abuse themselves and others. For some of these men, their abuser has found recovery, and together they have healed the relationship between them. Still, despite the healing of their specific relationship, the violent addict who tortured those men verbally, emotionally, and perhaps physically and/or sexually lives inside them. For over two decades I watched a man in recovery whose parents are also in recovery get honest in our men's retreat about his continuing pain from the abandonment and abuse that came from growing up with two alcoholic parents. He said, "I thought I dealt with all of this in the steps." The pain of past abuse and trauma is insidious and often beyond the capacity of twelve-step recovery *alone* to address. For many men, the abuser may be long dead but he or she continues to haunt him from the grave. That was the case for me for many years. I was only a year into recovery when my father died a tragic death due to his alcoholism.

My healing has come from two main sources. The first has been coming to understand trauma and doing the work to begin healing it. I had to develop the strength and courage to talk about all of the shame and pain that kept me silent for far too long. The second is that I have come to understand violence and abuse and what they look like in all of their various forms, and that I cocreated a standard of behavior for our home and our family. So, before we go any further, let's take some time to figure out how you understand violence right now.

Into Action

In your notebook, take four sheets of paper and set up four headings. For the first heading write *Physical Abuse.* The second heading is *Emotional Abuse,* the third is *Verbal Abuse,* and the final heading is *Sexual Abuse.* Now, on each of these pieces of paper write down a list of as many examples of each type of violence as you are able to come up with. You may want to do this exercise with your sponsor or some other men in recovery to help you come up with examples.

After you have completed the four lists, review the lists at the end of this chapter and compare them. Notice what you had that is not there and what you may have missed.

Outside of their physical forms, a lot of men have not really thought about what constitutes abuse and violence. The problem is that we almost never take the time to stop and have an open and honest conversation about it. We come by it very honestly since so much of how we are raised is in the context of violence—either the threat of violence or actual violence. We are surrounded by violence in our mass media: in the news, in movies, on television, and online. We are also taught the "zero sum" rule with respect to power. Either you have power over me or I have power over you. And if either of us becomes more powerful, it is inevitably at the other person's expense. This explains why victims of abuse may become perpetrators of abuse. Feeling weak and unmanly, the victim becomes aggressive or violent in an effort to reclaim strength and feel like a real man.

You have heard me talk about the challenges men have in creating healthy relationships in the context of the Rules. The Rules encourage disconnection and superficial relationships. I have also talked about the anger funnel and how men are consistently backed into an emotional corner because of how limited the emotional language and choices we have been given are. Now add in shame and perhaps trauma, and men don't know what to do with the inevitable vulnerabilities and uncomfortable (read "unmanly") feelings that arise in relationships.

Violence and abuse frequently occur when we aren't getting our needs met and are struggling in other ways in our relationships, and we don't know how to ask for help. We lack trust. We fear rejection. So we lash out in frustration. Or, we are in an unhealthy relationship but can't see that fact. We can only "feel" it. Rather than try to fix the relationship or leave in a healthy way, we act out violently to push the person away and end the relationship that way.

Most, though certainly not all, of the violence and abuse is committed by men—toward women, other men, and children. The interaction of gender and violence is one that has created a very complex dynamic between men and women. As a society we suffer from the delusion that women cannot be violent or abusive. There is a very complex dynamic in interpersonal violence (IPV) that takes place between human beings. A lot of people have attempted to oversimplify this, but there are no easy answers to abuse and violence. For those of us who have gotten stuck in the devastating cycle of trauma, shame, and violence and abuse, it takes time to separate those three and a lot of hard work—but it is possible, as many men have demonstrated.

Violence Against Women

Some of you are going to react as soon as you read this by saying, "What about violence against men?" We'll get there. But if men are ever going to feel safe in their relationships and be able to experience true intimacy, we have to understand how our ideas, beliefs, and behaviors affect our relationships with women. We have to understand how women experience us and how oblivious we so often are to that experience. We also have to understand how children experience us and how oblivious we often are to their experience, as well. The statistics are horrific. According to one study, every day at least three women (and one man) are killed by domestic violence. One study showed that one out of four women will experience domestic violence in her lifetime. I would go so far as to say the true number is more like three out of four when we begin to truly understand what violence looks like. This does not take into account all of the adult men who will also experience domestic violence in their lifetime. Violence is epidemic in our society, especially when you consider its more covert and indirect forms and how they show up in our day-to-day interactions.

First, we need to revisit some specific nuances of the Man Rules and how they affect our relationships with women and girls:

- The Rules are antifemininity.
- The Rules are about disconnection.
- The Rules pit men against each other.
- The Rules are often homophobic.
- The Rules discourage intimacy.
- The Rules do not allow for emotions other than anger.

The Rules help to shape the environment in which violence toward women happens. Some of it occurs in the context of seeing women as sex objects in combination with so many young men's desperate need to fit in and be accepted by other men, doing what the prevailing culture expects.

Power and Control

Have you ever thought about how central the idea of power is to your life? At the core of many Man Rules is the concept of power. While it seems to be an oversimplification of men's experience of shame to say that at its core is a fear of looking weak and doing everything we can not to look weak, there is no question that power and lack of power are central to male identity.

Interestingly, the twelve-step philosophy of recovery starts with the admission of our powerlessness in Step One, and continues with the ongoing acceptance of our lack of power and control. Then, in Step Two, we seek out a power greater than ourselves. Power and lack thereof is a central part of our recovery journey. With that in mind, how much time have you spent looking at your relationship to power and powerlessness? How have you reconciled that with your ideas of being a man?

As I mentioned earlier, one of the ideas that my training partner Rick talks about is how our interest in power and control is natural and has positive aspects. Imagine what your life would look like without some degree of healthy power and control. It would be a mess. Anyone who attempts to tell you otherwise is setting you up. With good intentions, many people and programs think that men's attempts to exert power and control over others (usually because they are scared, ashamed, and/ or traumatized) are inherently bad, and so they send the message to men that there is something inherently wrong with power and control. "You have to let go of control" and "Let go and let God." Such pithy sayings can be misinterpreted to mean that there is something inherently wrong with control.

Men need to look at how we view power and control. If you're in recovery, you have admitted you are powerless over your addiction. Great! That is a good start. Are you able to admit that you are powerless over a lot of other things in your life? How do you respond to feeling powerless? How much effort have you put into really looking at how you relate to power and powerlessness?

It may be less about noticing how power shows up in your life as much as noticing how you feel and react to the experience of being powerless. Powerlessness is not a manly concept. It often doesn't feel good. You experience people and situations over which you are powerless multiple times every day. How does that affect you? I am not a fan of feeling powerless at all. The truth is that the spiritual principle of powerlessness or surrender is essential not only to recovery, but to our lives as men. The more we move into our recovery, the more we begin to embrace the inherent powerlessness of our lives. The beauty is that the more we are able to see all of the areas in which we are powerless, the more we are also able to see all of the areas where we have genuine personal power. In order to do this we have to reconcile our views on power and powerlessness with our ideas about being men.

Another important concept is that of power *with* versus power *over.* I talked about this in detail in Step One of *A Man's Way through the Twelve Steps.* As I said there, "As long as you are using power and control to dominate your relationships, you will never have the love and closeness you seek." Men tend to see power as something that has to be exercised over people. In order for me to have power, it must be mine—it cannot be shared. How can it be power if you have to share it?

The truth is that until we shed our shame about being perceived as weak, our efforts at gaining power almost always backfire in unhealthy ways. One of the beauties of the Twelve Steps is that they teach us a new way to explore power, and this starts with Step One, with the concept of powerlessness over our addiction. How can it be that this thing that is destroying us can be overcome by ceasing to fight it—by surrendering? How unmanly is that? Surrender is a very vulnerable experience, typically associated with weakness. Yet we also find that the admission of powerlessness gives us power. When we know to stop fighting against an unbeatable foe, then we can put our energy toward what we actually have power over. If you think about it, the concept of a Higher Power, while it is a power greater than us, is the quintessential relationship of "power with." By doing our part in partnership with our Higher Power—going to meetings, reaching out for help, and talking about our problems—we get the power we need to live productive lives and create and maintain healthy relationships with others. Through those actions of perceived weakness, we gain strength and demonstrate courage.

The paradox is that genuine power comes from letting go of the need to feel powerful through domination and control. Sometimes when a man admits powerlessness over his addiction, he attempts to fortify the rest of his life as if he is saying, "Yes, I am powerless over my addiction, so I need to make sure I am powerful everywhere else, or what kind of man does that make me?" We don't say this consciously, but it is there for a lot of us, and it tracks back to the Man Rules. The key for men is to see that the principle of powerlessness does not just apply to recovery, it applies to life. It especially applies to our relationships.

Abuse of Men

There is no way to talk about violence and abuse and not talk about the abuse that men suffer: at the hands of other men, as well as women; as boys in the home, at school, in the community, and in our homes from our partners. You cannot talk about men's trauma without talking about the connection to the abuse of boys and young men. We have millions of men walking around wounded from the trauma of how they were treated as children and adolescents. I firmly believe that the abuse of boys is deeply connected to how we train them to become men—and the ripple effects hurt a lot of people.

The abuse of males has been a poorly addressed topic. Almost every single man I interviewed had some abuse in his history. Some of the examples are horrific. None of it is okay. We have systematically accepted and even endorsed the abuse of boys, and then we are surprised when men act out with abuse and violence. Let's not even talk about the various systems like the juvenile justice and criminal justice systems in which boys and men find themselves disproportionately represented, especially boys and men of color. The amount of abuse and retraumatization that those individuals experience within those systems is catastrophic. Furthermore, as I'll talk about later in the book, there is still widespread mistreatment of boys and men who do not identify and present as heterosexual. This abuse comes from their families, their schoolmates, the religious community, and others. Boys who do not act masculine enough are frequently ostracized, bullied, and even beaten.

Below are just some of the answers the men gave to my questions about their experience with the different types of abuse (physical, verbal, emotional, and sexual). This is another place where you might want to take a deep breath. I share this not to trigger you or to overwhelm you but to paint a picture of the powerful and insidious histories of abuse that men are walking around with, so often in silence because they are deeply ashamed and never feel safe enough to share it:

- "I was beaten severely by my adopted mother and my stepfather."
- "Until my dad sobered up at my age sixteen, it was a bit rough. Punishment was with a belt or a shaved baseball bat. A few rages from drinking brought a few fistfights as well."
- "Therapy taught me that what I believed was my strategic hooking up as a teenager was really perpetration by older men. It was confusing to learn, but now I have a better understanding."
- "I was sexually abused when I was young by an older neighborhood boy."
- "I was sexually abused by a scoutmaster for about six years. It completely messed up my view of sex and my understanding of how relationships are formed."
- "Torture would more accurately describe it. The reservation and boarding school almost destroyed me."
- "Mom was a rager and dad was nonconfrontational; we just weren't ever safe or at peace in our home."
- "Watching the abuse in the house growing up caused some deep pain for me. The yelling was tough, but I did have to deal with (in my Fourth Step) the abuse my dad caused with my mom."
- "Being described as worthless and good-for-nothing was heard for too long for me not to believe it today. I am constantly trying to prove myself or prove that I am lovable."

I also asked these men how the effects of the abuse have shown up in their recovery. Remember, the average amount of time in recovery for this group is about twenty years. They are men who have done a lot of deep work to heal. Take another deep breath:

- "I never wanted anyone to touch me."
- "I didn't trust men."
- "I had difficulty trusting and connecting in relationships."
- "I have always struggled with anger, yelling, punching walls, etc. . . . even in early recovery."
- "Being a dad, in my mind I will think about physically hurting my kids, spankings, slappings, etc. I am sure that is the imprint I have."
- "I believed I was worthless."
- "I avoided sexual contact with women, and then women were the object of my sexuality."
- "Being sexually abused altered my understanding of how relationships were formed and grew, what integrity and being a man meant, and because the abuser in my situation was the scout leader and a close friend of our family, this was made worse. This continues to show up in relationships in my recovery, even after spending significant time processing it. I tend to want to use sex to defuse stressful or tension-filled situations. I look to sex as a way to get approval. My substance use was very connected with this abuse, and separating the two has been a major challenge."
- "Did not deserve to be loved."
- "I've just had a lot to process from that. Sixteen years in [recovery] and I'm still working on my fear, PTSD, and not strategizing on how to be a good kid to avoid consequences."
- "Anger management is my issue. I have the capacity to take the air out of a room in an argument, a debate, or a public disagreement."
- "There is part of my head that thinks that verbal abuse helped me, and I have to correct that thinking on a regular basis. I have caught myself being verbally abusive to others, fortunately often enough with time to make amends. I also have a pattern of searching out authority figures professionally who motivate through verbal abuse."

This is just a small glimpse into the lasting legacy of the abuse that men experience. You may have had similar experiences. Maybe you swore you would never tell anyone about it. Maybe you have minimized it, saying it wasn't a big deal. Maybe you told someone and they didn't believe you. Maybe someone said or implied that it was your fault. Maybe you have been told all your life that what happened to you doesn't happen to boys or men. Maybe you're just scared. What matters is right now. What do you need to feel safe enough to bring your pain out into the light? You deserve peace. You deserve to be free.

What happens when we stop using substances or mood-altering behaviors to occupy our thoughts and energy? All of this ugliness starts to come to the surface, and we have nothing to deaden the pain. The more coping mechanisms we take out of our lives (food, sex, work, rage, coffee/energy drinks, smoking, excessive medication, and all of the other kinds of escape and drama), the more we are left with the pain, the discomfort, the anxiety, and the silence, which isn't silent at all.

Because of how boys and men are socialized to view power and because of the emotional restraints placed on us early in our lives, men tend to identify with the abuser. It makes complete sense: Would you rather feel powerful or powerless? Doesn't there come a time when you are tired of feeling powerless and you just want to feel powerful or simply safe? When you are getting beaten up or being told that you are a piece of shit, how good does it feel to fight back, or find someone even less powerful than you? The saddest thing is that when so many boys and young men finally fight back or fight others, they also set themselves on the trajectory to becoming that which they hate. This is all part of the hard conversation that we have to have if we want to end the cycles of violence tearing our relationships and our communities apart. So many boys grow into the men they never wanted to be. The Rules combined with abuse and trauma is a tragic and toxic mix.

Compassion *and* Accountability

When it comes to understanding and intervening on male violence, we tend to take one of two approaches—compassion or accountability. Neither of these approaches alone has proven to be very effective. The compassion approach is where we see wounded men who are acting out of those wounds and causing deep pain for others. A lot of men's work focuses on this aspect of the issue without emphasizing enough how important it is for men to understand the full impact of their behavior on others and that healing their wounds is necessary but not enough. Drawing solid and firm lines that men cannot cross is an essential part of the healing process, especially when it comes to healing relationships.

The accountability approach is the standard operating philosophy in court-ordered treatment for domestic violence and anger management. Its essence is that the man is the perpetrator and that the victim of violence is the most important person and almost always a woman. In this paradigm, while it may not be stated explicitly, men are bad people who need to get good, rather than sick people who need to get well. Another reality that rarely receives attention is that there are some wounded people working in the field of domestic violence treatment who embrace this philosophy, in part because it allows them to (often subconsciously) exact some kind of psychological revenge on perpetrators in their own lives. There people working in the domestic violence field who need as much love and support as any of the men they are attempting to help. There are also many wonderful people who genuinely want to help men and women whose lives are being destroyed by the pernicious cycle of violence, but work in a system that seems to have a structural bias.

The answer, if it is not obvious, is that there has to be a balanced approach that brings compassion together with accountability, which should really be termed responsibility because of how often accountability is paired with power over and/or punishment. In this paradigm, the focus is on the wounds you carry that contribute to your behavior while you recognize that the behavior is unacceptable and will not be tolerated. It is best exemplified in the statement we recommend every program that uses our work display on their group room walls: *"Whatever happened to you as a child was not your fault; if you are engaged in any kind of abusive behavior, you are 100 percent responsible for your actions and it must stop."* It is important for men to hear this message consistently, lovingly, and firmly.

Why is this important to you? Because if you struggle with being verbally, emotionally, physically, and/or sexually abusive, you have to find the ability to internalize this philosophy for yourself and begin to take personal responsibility. I find that most men need to spend more time cultivating compassion for themselves than accountability. The accountability part tends to come pretty easily to us. Perhaps a bit too easily. It certainly is a masculine quality connected to discipline, integrity, and responsibility. But compassion for ourselves? That is a much harder place to go because it requires us to truly see ourselves as wounded, and that means getting vulnerable. It is easy to pretend that compassion is not something we need. But men who are not able to practice compassion for themselves slowly die inside.

Feeling sorry for myself is far different from having compassion for myself. Making excuses for my behavior is obviously not compassionate. True compassion stems from the ability to step back from the pain. Compassion literally means "to suffer with." If that is the case, then compassion for self is a delicate dance, particularly as it relates to violence and abuse. I began to cultivate compassion for myself when I was able, without sliding into the victim mentality, to acknowledge all of the pain I experienced as a child and how much that hurt my spirit, while at the same time being responsible for my best behavior in my present relationships. I made and continue to make mistakes, and that is why ongoing compassion is so important to nurture. We need to learn how to allow ourselves to make mistakes without beating the crap out of ourselves.

When we practice true compassion for ourselves, particularly related to pain we may have experienced in our childhood, we become fiercely committed to ensuring we do not do the same things to our children or anyone else. I have watched this happening in my relationship with Grace. There have been times when I have felt "it" all rise inside me and I want to crush her. I hate to admit it. That wounded kid inside me doesn't like kids who act out or are really emotional to not get put down, shut down, or knocked down. That is a powerful force that is so important to notice and to accept. It may not make sense at first glance, but I have come to realize that the best way to not let that negative and abusive energy affect my interactions with Grace, Nancy, and others is to honor it and notice that it is a sign that I am not taking care of myself in some way.

Hurt People, Hurt People

I will never forget mentioning this saying to a colleague at work, who replied, "What is that, some kind of cheer?" as he pumped his fist above his head and repeated the phrase several times. We are such a reactive society. Hurt others before they hurt you! Hurt others because you have been hurt. Hurt others because you are hurting. We are emotionally disconnected. The truth is that we tend to stop hurting others when we stop hurting. We often stop hurting when we stop hurting others. They are both essential to healing.

This has been a long journey for me, one that I will be on for the rest of my life. The first thing I had to do was to recognize my lack of understanding about violence. Similar to the exercise I asked that you do earlier in this chapter, I had to begin to understand the connection between the violence I experienced as a child and adolescent and the violence and abuse I was perpetuating in my life and my relationships. I went to my first anger management program when I had about four years in recovery and was with guys who had beaten their wives, one of whom had literally attacked his wife with a crowbar. I thought to myself, "Thank God I'm not like *those* men!" I had convinced myself that I wasn't violent because I wasn't beating women or hitting kids. I wasn't acting out violently against other men. Or so I thought. I left there learning very little and still not ready to deal with how rage was affecting my life. The staff running that program NEVER talked about trauma and seemed to have no understanding of it.

I felt so much powerlessness, fear, and shame in my life on a daily basis that I couldn't see my behavior and what everyone else was seeing: short-tempered, vindictive reactions to any perceived insult, gossiping, raging, yelling, biting sarcasm, and other completely unacceptable behaviors toward people, especially those I had determined to be weaker than me, and often those closest to me. I do not even want to talk about how I treated my mother, who had already suffered so much abuse from my father. If these targeted others were not weaker than me, I constantly felt threatened and plotted my revenge.

The term "anger management" itself is inherently flawed. It implies that anger is the problem rather than a symptom. It is a falsehood that we need to manage our anger. Managing your drinking does not keep you sober. Managing your gambling does not keep you from blowing your monthly salary one more time. Managing your use of massage parlors does not keep you from acting out. The First Step says that our lives have become unmanageable, not that we have to now manage the problem. You may think I am overstating this issue, but the power of language is not to be underestimated.

We do not need to manage our anger—we need to address our shame, deal with our trauma, grow and practice our emotional awareness, and manage our inappropriate behavior, including behavior driven by our anger. I have learned to use my anger and upset feelings as a signal. For instance, I know if I start saying the "F" word or I am short with family members or our dog, I am not in a good place. If I am preoccupied with other people's behavior and want to make them the problem, I need to look inside myself. I have a whole list of behaviors, body sensations, and thought patterns that I know contribute to my moving down a path toward rage and abusiveness. Those are the things I need to pay close attention to and manage, with the support and love of others, as best I am able.

The next part of the journey for me was that I had to accept the fact that as a result of the home that I grew up in I did not have the greatest understanding of what would be considered peaceful and creating safety. One of the lessons I had internalized was that if someone loves you, they hurt you. We never talked about violence or abuse in my house, so it meant it wasn't there. My dad just had a bad temper. Why? Because I was such a difficult kid. Because I didn't listen. Because I was such a behavior problem. As I said earlier, I did not begin to appreciate the chaos and violence I grew up in until I encountered something different and could not handle it. I consistently tried to re-create that chaos and dysfunction in my living environment and in my relationships.

Then, I had to have an open dialogue with Nancy and others, like my sponsor and close friends, about this issue. I needed to learn to be open to honest feedback from Nancy and those who truly do have an understanding of what it looks like to live in a peaceful and safe place. Nancy grew up in that kind of environment, and she was trying to re-create *it* in our family. It took the longest time for me to trust what she was saying, mostly from the shame I would feel when I acted out. She "didn't get it." She was overreacting. She refused to look at her own behavior. I wasn't willing or able to listen to her. Some of it was because of the mental distortions that came with the intense traumatic reactions I would have. Some of it was the intense shame in knowing on some level that I was not acting like the man I truly wanted to be. "I am not the enemy," Nancy would say over and over again. That was the hardest thing for me to understand—it felt like she was out to hurt me, and so I had to protect myself. I could not trust her. I had to hurt her. The first time I was able to withstand her holding my hands, looking into my eyes, and saying that phrase, it felt worse than getting punched. It told me how incredibly hard it has been to allow myself to be loved and to let love in. I feel sad writing that right now because of how long it has taken for me to simply learn how to be loved and love others.

Finally, I have had to push myself to be as accountable as I can be to be true to my own ideal of peace and safety. That means being able to see, and be told about, all of the ways I am not being peaceful and safe. I have had to dig as deep as I can to cocreate that in my home. What this means is that I have had to make a lot of apologies. I am constantly failing *and* improving in this effort. Grace and I even learned to sing the same song together: *If you feel so mad, and you want to roar!*

Take a deep breath and count to four . . . 1, 2, 3, 4!

Especially for Grace's sake, I have had to become super responsible for how I express myself in our home. It means allowing a four-year-old to be a four-year-old and allowing her to be emotional, sensitive, and irrational. It often means making amends.

What's So Funny About Peace, Love, and Understanding?

The answer to the above question is "nothing." Not a thing. In the end, it is what we all seek. And most of us want to give it to others despite all of the times that we don't do it. In my first year of recovery I wore a shirt all the time. It said in big letters on the front, PEACE. What I did not understand or was not willing to admit was how little peace I had in my life or in my heart. I was a deeply hurting, angry, and confused young man. I had no peace, and that was precisely why I was advertising it so strongly—"Look at me! I believe in peace!" when it was more like "Help me, I need PEACE!"

I believe all men have an obligation to:

- Take a stand for peace in our homes and communities.
- Admit to and own the shadow parts of ourselves that seek power and control as a way to dominate and control others.
- Understand what violence is in all of its complexities and nuances.
- Look as honestly as we possibly can at our violence and how we have been and are violent and abusive in our relationships— and change our behavior.
- Talk to our loved ones about violence and abuse and even ask them how they may have experienced us.
- Speak out against violence against women, children, and men. (I often don't hear enough people who are supposedly against violence being as vocal about violence against men as they are with respect to women and children.)
- Challenge and confront men, women, and children who act out violently and abusively with both compassion and strong expectations for personal responsibility.

To me these are nonnegotiable. If you want to be a man of principle, these are part of the agreement. It is one of the few times you will hear me say how I think a man *should* show up as a man. You cannot be serious about your recovery and committed to your relationships and not endorse these qualities.

Nothing hurts more than a look of fear or hurt in a child's face when you know you have caused it out of your own shame. My hope is that my admitting this here might make it easier for you to admit some of the hard truths about this topic to yourself and to those you love. We will not have peace in our lives and in our homes until we learn to tell the truth about all the places where peace and safety do not exist.

The danger for many men is in comparing our behavior to the more extreme cases. Maybe you have acted in extreme ways. If so, you really need to talk to someone about it and get support. Maybe your behavior is more subtle and not overtly abusive. That does not mean it doesn't affect the degree of safety and peace in the home. Just remember that when I talk about my struggles I am not saying I was beating my girlfriends—it means that as a result of my trauma and toxic shame continually being triggered, I misused power and control in an attempt to keep myself safe. It worked in some ways, but at a great cost to me and those closest to me. I have watched the veil of denial fall away from so many men as they have been challenged to move away from simply talking about "anger and resentment" and see with open eyes the effects of their behavior on others.

The key is to look at it as honestly as you are able. If you simply conclude that your home is a peaceful and a safe home without asking specifically where it might not be safe or peaceful, you are like the guy who decides he doesn't have trauma without being willing to look at that possibility. Don't let fear prevent you from being thorough in taking a look at where your home and your relationships might not be as safe and peaceful as they can be. Have the conversation with your loved ones and see what they have to say. Talk to men you can trust about everything that is happening in your relationships. You also get to give your input. This isn't about your partner telling you how you are behaving, it is about people who love each other coming together to really reflect on their lives and the degree of peace and safety they feel, want, and are willing to cocreate in their lives.

The Different Types of Violence

Physical Abuse: pinching, slapping, punching, pushing, hair pulling, spitting, restraining, shaking, kicking, choking, dragging, ripping clothing, biting, throwing objects, reckless driving with a passenger, hitting with objects, blocking (a person's exit or entrance), preventing someone from calling the police, using your body to intimidate, punching or kicking walls or doors, slamming objects or walls or doors, burning, stabbing.

Emotional Abuse: silence, withdrawing, withholding approval or affection, manipulation through dishonesty, intimidation, not acknowledging the other person's feelings.

Verbal Abuse: name-calling, ridicule, constant criticism, blaming, threatening, shouting or screaming.

Sexual Abuse: telling jokes, harassment, violating another's boundaries, giving inappropriate information, inappropriate touching, voyeurism, sexual hugs, commenting on developing bodies, reading or viewing pornography with a child, exhibitionism, fondling, French-kissing a child, oral sex, penetration.

Into Action

The most important thing I can say here is that if you are engaged in any abusive behavior, please get help. If you are in a relationship where someone else is engaging in abusive behavior against you or someone else you care about, especially children, please get help. If you find yourself consistently thinking about the abusive and traumatic experiences you've had, whether as a child, adolescent, and/or adult, please get help and support to understand how those experiences are affecting you and your relationships. For any of these scenarios, this is where a good trauma therapist could be extremely helpful (for more information on this, see Chapter Thirteen, Healing Trauma).

► Referring to the lists you wrote out about the different types of abuse, choose three that you witnessed and/or experienced growing up from a caregiver, sibling, or friend, or from another situation. What was it like for you to experience it? What do you think was going on with the person who acted abusively?

► Looking at the lists again, choose three that you have engaged in. For each one, answer the following:
  • What was *really* going on with you in that situation?
  • What do you think it was like for the person you were being abusive toward?
  • What is it like for you thinking about it now?
  • What would you want to do differently now?

Advanced Into Action

► Ask your partner to look at the lists of the four different types of abuse. Ask them which ones they have experienced from you and how it has felt for them. *If this feels like too sensitive a topic to address face-to-face, perhaps ask them to write it down, or you can have the discussion on this with your couples counselor.*

► Share with your partner what you are reading about in this chapter and ask their permission to share with them which types of abuse you feel you have experienced from them, as well as what it has been like for you and how you would like to address any such behavior in the future.

CHAPTER TEN
Sex and Sexuality

"There seems to be a huge difference between having sex and making love. Having sex is easy. Making love is like jumping over the Grand Canyon." –Randy

Healthy Sexuality

No book about men and relationships would be worth much without a chapter exploring sex and sexuality. Each man's sexuality is his own. It is a very personal and sacred part of who we are. I honor that and encourage you to do the same for yourself. Let me be the first to say that I am a neophyte in this area. It took me many years to get to the point where I fully understood that the act of sex is just a small part of the relationship and of our sexuality. In *Helping Men Recover,* we use the definition of sexuality that comes out of Dr. Stephanie Covington's expertise: "the physical, emotional, social, and spiritual parts of ourselves integrated into our identities and ways of living." According to the Sexual Health Model, also used in *Helping Men Recover,* there are ten components to creating a healthy sexuality:

1. Talking about sex
2. Culture and sexual identity
3. Sexual anatomy and functioning

4. Sexual healthcare and safer sex
5. Challenges: overcoming barriers to sexual health
6. Body image
7. Masturbation and fantasy
8. Positive sexuality
9. Intimacy and relationships
10. Spirituality

This list is included so that you can use it as a checklist in developing your own healthy sexuality. Men often joke about sex, and our public bravado often belies our insecurity, confusion, and shame. Sex is a barometer for the relationship. That is where understanding our sexuality comes into play. When we see the act of sex as part of a much greater whole, everything changes. When we are doing well emotionally and spiritually and when we are truly connected to our partner, the sex is great—explosive, connected, open, adventurous, and deeply intimate.

Roland said it well: "It's probably one of the biggest secrets in recovery, i.e., men's sexual acting out/fantasies/behavior, etc. I think sex is one of the most predictable ways that men compromise their recovery principles and values." I remember attending a workshop on young people in recovery at an international recovery conference in Minneapolis, where I heard a young guy speak so beautifully about his recovery and how the principles were transforming his life. That night I went to a party on the Mississippi River and saw that same young man coming out of the woods with a young woman. She went over to her group of friends and he walked over to his friends next to me, telling them, "Oh man . . . I just got my dick sucked by that hot newcomer. She's definitely going to stay sober now!" He laughed, and they laughed with him. As I looked over toward her I saw what seemed to be a very uneasy smile. As the other guys in his group, other supposed leaders of the young people in recovery, high-fived him, he proceeded to share some of the details. I walked away, disgusted and deeply disappointed. My guess is that the guy was a much better man than his behavior in that moment, but that nobody called him on it. And we don't—there is far too much silence and collusion in the twelve-step community among men regarding our sexual behavior and our immature concepts of sexuality. Jim said, "I think sex f#$@s us up more than anything else in recovery. We need to address sexuality and the connected behavior directly if we are to recover."

More than anything, we have to go beyond the idea that sex is only about sex acts. We overuse the anthropological justification for male hypersexuality that men are biologically driven to be promiscuous and women to be monogamous. From the perspective of evolution there may be some truth to that, but to say that it determines our choices and behavior today is foolish and a B.S. excuse that does a great disservice to men. The truth is that infidelity for men usually is a function of shame and insecurity. It is also a way for men to avoid getting too close to someone and to protect themselves from the discomfort of intimacy and vulnerability, particularly when trauma is involved. What goes on for most men beneath the surface of infidelity or involvement in multiple romantic relationships can be very different from what we tend to assume.

Since entering recovery, every man I interviewed for this book, regardless of sexual orientation, reported that sex for them included intimacy and connection. In fact, that was one of the most significant changes instigated by their recovery that the men identified in their responses to the questions in my survey: Sex was much more than just a selfish act about them "getting off." Are we to believe that these men are so different from other men? Jim, who just happens to be gay, said this: "I had to look at sex in a more honest way after getting sober, and one of the realizations for me has been that sex is better when it is shared with someone I have feelings for and share life with. Anonymous sex could be enjoyable as an experience, but afterward I did not like the way I felt."

The lie, reinforced by the Man Rules, is that men only think about sex, and our only interest in intimacy is through sex. We are taught very early that emotional intimacy is for girls and sex will make you a man. That lie has destroyed many men's relationships and left us disconnected and unfulfilled.

We are also socialized to believe that women have something that men want and we have to work to get "it." We have to treat them nicely, we have to pretend that we are sensitive and have feelings, we have to act cool, and even say "those three words," all to get sex. It's a game that has been shown in hundreds of movies. And women are complicit in this dynamic as well, through flirtatious behavior, expecting men to buy them meals and presents, and sending mixed messages because of their own conflicts (I want to have sex but don't want be called a slut, easy, promiscuous, etc.).

Helping men understand relationships is about expanding what they believe is possible. Luke, a recovering sex addict, has had to look at these issues in depth as a result of his addiction: "I had poor sexual boundaries with others before recovery. Since recovery from sex addiction, I see sex and my sexuality in the following way: (1) My sexuality is NOT an option. It is a gift and a blessing from my Creator. (2) Being sexual (or expressing myself sexually) *is* optional. I won't die if I don't have sex with myself or someone else." The solution he has found seems to speak for most of the men I interviewed, whether they identified as sex addicts or not, because in the end it is about creating a healthy sexuality.

Many of us men are confused about our sexuality and the appropriate role of sex in a relationship. The Rules have really done a number on us when it comes to sex. Are we over-sexed animals, slaves to our testosterone? No, but we were very young when we first got the message that sex is extremely important, and we kept getting that message. Like a lot of boys, I was very young (seven years old) when I saw my first pornographic magazine. From that moment, particularly because my parents knew nothing about it, I had a corrupted and confused idea about sex, sexuality, and women. One of the men, now in his twenty-third year of recovery, who has been doing extensive trauma work shared with me his recent realization of the trauma he experienced watching a very explicit pornographic film and the effect that had on him as a child growing up in a violent and strict religious environment. Those experiences came together to create some very painful and unhealthy sexual behaviors long into his recovery. He is far from alone.

For many men, the way they first learned about sex was at the hands of an older child or adult who forced them to do and experience things sexually that ripped away a part of their soul. About one-third of the men I interviewed identified some form of sexual abuse in their history, far greater than the "one in six" statistic commonly cited for the general population. I cannot overstate the impact sexual abuse has on a man's life and his relationships. Issues like hypersexuality, fear of sex, erectile dysfunction, and many others can plague a man and keep him from being able to develop relationships with true intimacy and connection. Many survivors of sexual trauma have intense reactions—often as confusing to them as to anyone they are with—to anything sexual. Frequently these men retreat from sex because they equate it with very negative experiences (violence, shame, abuse, secrets, control, domination, etc.).

For other men, their first experience with sex was tainted when their own parents' shame clashed against innocent attempts to explore their sexuality, either by themselves or with a friend. For me, it was the fact that my body felt completely defective. For several years, while other boys reached puberty and talked more and more about their nascent sexual experiences, I felt great shame, not only for not having had sex, but for literally not being able to. By the time I did hit puberty, it was too late—the damage was done. The bottom line here is that surface appearances and behaviors can be extremely deceiving, for many men have considerable confusion and pain regarding sex and sexuality.

So let's go back to the Man Rules. Among the Rules is that we are at our manliest when we are "conquering" women—when we are having as much sex as possible with as many of the hot women as possible. Think of all the other Rules inherent in that one Rule:

- Don't be gay.
- Only have sex with beautiful women.
- Always be available for sex.
- You better be able to get an erection (erectile dysfunction [ED] was previously known as impotence—as in not having power).
- Sex is about performance.
- Women are sex objects, there for our pleasure.
- If you are having sex with hot women, you are a man. If you are not, well . . .

Homophobia

The term *homophobia* was originally created to define the irrational fear or hatred of homosexuals, but it really seems to go beyond that.

Homophobia is really about men's fear of men—homosexuality is just the tip of the iceberg. It certainly is a major factor in preventing us from having the kind of relationships with other men that are possible, and that so many of us, both straight and gay, want. The difference to keep in mind when thinking of our gay brothers is that while both gay and straight men may get ridiculed for being emotional and sensitive, in 2014 there are still men being ostracized, ridiculed, beaten, and even killed for being gay.

Men, gay and straight, realize that the kind of support and connection we used to think we could only get from women we can also get from men. Jim, a gay man, voiced something that I also connected to earlier in my recovery: "I have fewer women friends in recovery than I did before I got sober. I had bought into gay stereotypes and had lots of 'girlfriends.' As my trust level for men has grown in recovery, I find that I have more male friends." The key is allowing ourselves to connect with those men, and for a lot of us (gay or straight) it means being honest and accountable for the homophobia that has corroded our relationships with men, and walking through it.

David talked about being in a world where one can be hated and judged for who he is. David has it twice as difficult because he is gay and African-American. I see my own homophobia rise to the surface at times, and I have to be aware of it without shame or I will miss the opportunity to see it and do something different. If I feel shame about it and cannot talk about it with men I can trust, I will continue to separate myself from others. One of the beautiful parts of the twelve-step community is that I have never seen a group of men more able to transcend the superficial labels and categories in which we place human beings.

My first best friend in recovery is a gay man, Gary, one of the interviewees for this book. One of the most important lessons he taught me was how unimportant his being gay was to our friendship, especially as we grabbed onto each other to make it through our first year of recovery. I learned a lot about my ignorance and how deeply it ran. I was also able to see that my fear of gay men had nothing to do with them and everything to do with my incredible lack of comfort with myself, my sexuality, and my sense of being a man.

When men become healthy, they begin to think, talk, and act differently about sex. You can't mature as a man and not reflect on how sex fits into the bigger picture of your life. Mike talked about this: "I had no idea what being a sexual man was before I got sober. It was about fulfilling my wants/desires and to hell with anything and anyone else. As my shame has reduced, as I've learned to identify and share feelings, and as I now understand intimacy, I have a more mature and rewarding sex life." Becoming a healthy man in our modern society involves looking at your sexual ideas and behaviors. Examining this area of your life by taking a regular inventory is a really good idea. This is another benefit of rigorously working the Twelve Steps. When you do a thorough sexual inventory as part of the Fourth and Fifth Steps, you have to look in all of the dark corners: pornography, fear of sex, sexual abuse, nonconsensual sex, objectification of women, sex for money/drugs, homophobia, and so on. Your ability to maintain your recovery may depend on whether or not you grow in your understanding of sexuality and how it fits into your life.

The Sex Funnel

This section is about a core concept from our curriculum, *Helping Men Recover,* describing the vehicle through which so many men experience *all* forms of intimacy. After I learned about the anger funnel, it was apparent to me that there is a "sex funnel" as well. When feelings of closeness, affection, attraction, love, and connection pass through the sex funnel, they become interpreted through the lens of sex. We are mostly unconscious of it, but it affects much of how we behave in relationships. Nate talked about it this way: "The easiest thing is talking about the act of sex. The hardest thing is to talk about true intimacy, feeling loved and desired, and other components of healthy sexuality."

Sex Funnel

Attraction
Intimacy
Love
Closeness
Affection

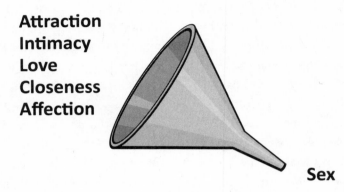

Sex

If you are a heterosexual man, how many times have you felt close to another man and held back from expressing those feelings? Said differently, how many men, regardless of sexual identity, feel attraction to or affection for a man and recoil or instinctively distance themselves, if only momentarily, from the man because they are not able to separate the feeling of affection or closeness from sex? For some men it is not momentary, but rather a constant saboteur of their relationships with other men, keeping them at arm's distance or more. This is not a cognitive experience—it is rooted inside us and operates on a visceral level. But it is there for many of us, keeping us from experiencing the depth and power of connections with other men—which means it also affects our relationships with women because of the incredible pressure it puts on them to carry the weight of intimacy and emotional expression. Everybody loses out.

Women are also impacted by the idea of the sex funnel, but their experience of it is different. I don't know how much of it is nature and how much is nurture, but when I was getting married the couple leading our marriage class told us, "Women have sex when they feel loved and men feel loved when they have sex." That remains true for me, but not nearly as much as it once was. This idea resonates with other men I have spoken to as well, though they also described it as being much truer for them prior to recovery. Once you begin to connect with all of the elements of intimacy before they go into the sex funnel, you see what Luke has discovered: "I am more present when being sexual with my wife. It's less about what I'm going to get from her and what I can give to her. Snuggling in bed with my wife, holding her hand while walking, singing with her, or just plain sharing something fun with her is sometimes preferable or more powerful than being sexual with her."

It takes a real man to admit that. Ricardo said it very simply: "I no longer have 'just sex.' I can feel everything now." The difference for me today is that I am aware of the sex funnel operating in my life. I can feel loved outside of sex. I am learning how important it is for me to allow myself to let Nancy's love in without connecting it to sex at all.

The Rules train us to objectify others. Sometimes it happens when thoughts of sex just seem to pop up, and when sexual feelings interfere with or otherwise change the quality of our interactions. Naturally, sexual thoughts and feelings are going to come up at times, and there is nothing wrong with that, but when we attach to them and they slip into the funnel, our focus becomes distorted and single-minded. When we create a space for men to talk about this issue, it is amazing how many men can see how often it operates in their lives.

My personal experience has been that having an awareness of the sex funnel and noticing when basic feelings of connection and intimacy are about to slide into its narrow and limiting confines, I can simply be with the feelings without judgment. This practice works with my wife as much as it does with women I meet in the trainings I conduct and conferences I attend. Whether it is thinking that sex is the connection I need from my wife or thinking that a woman who is attractive is worth more of my time than a woman I don't find attractive, I am constantly navigating the impact of the sex funnel. Sex alone cannot create the connections I desire. When I don't allow myself the full spectrum of feelings of intimacy I limit my relationships with women and men alike, and when that happens I limit my experience of life.

Sex Will Not Save Your Life

If I tell you that sometimes it can feel like sex will save your life, you might say, "That is silly, Dan." If that statement doesn't ring true for you, then try the opposite. How do you feel when you do not have sex? How do you feel if you perceive sexual rejection by your partner? How often do you use sex to fill some other need? If you are anything like me, it is probably a lot. Despite how much more aware I am of my tendency to look toward Nancy for sex when I really need something else, I still do it. What is the alternative? If I sit long enough with the discomfort I am feeling, I usually come to the realization that it has nothing to do with sex, or even with her.

The truth is that if your partner thinks you are only interested in being with them if it is going to lead to sex, or that you are only interested in getting off and are less concerned about their sexual needs and wants, they will disconnect. Josh said, "It's important to be in the mind-set of giving and connecting." Important, yes, but not always that easy. If the only channel for our sexuality is sex, our partners will start to push away, and without knowing what is happening, we personalize it without really looking at our part. Then perhaps we shut down or start acting out sexually in other ways. In any event, communication ceases.

If you are unaware of this process or unable to talk to your partner about it, you will likely continue to operate as if sex is going to solve your problems and save your life. This is like drinking water because you can't breathe—it only makes the problem worse. But when you do begin to do things differently, it will mean not only improved intimacy but better and more fulfilling sex as well. Bobby said it beautifully, especially from the perspective of those of us grounded in the Twelve Steps: "Sex without intimacy is like sobriety without spirituality. It just ain't. Intimacy is the goal; sex is a healthy expression, just one expression, of true intimacy."

Cuddling? Really?

One of the hardest sentences for me to write in *A Man's Way through the Twelve Steps* was about how sometimes I just wanted Nancy to hold me. After ten years of marriage believing that cuddling was nothing more than Nancy's lack of interest in sex, I realized there is something very special about cuddling. The first thing I realized about cuddling was that it really does have its place. Call it cuddling or just lying with each other, nonerotic touching, caressing, sitting close together watching TV. Call it whatever you want, but it isn't about sex. It is about connection. It sends the message to both partners that the love you profess to have goes beyond just having someone to fill your sexual needs.

When men begin to give themselves permission to cuddle, they give themselves permission to have needs for connection beyond sex. Every man has them, but they can be very hard to identify and admit, especially under the influence of the Rules. And let's be honest; once you have an erection, there can be a sense of urgency that can feel overpowering: *I must be relieved!* Actually, it is a very powerful discipline to not let the "little head" do all the thinking. To be able to get sexually aroused and accept that this can be its own experience and it doesn't always have to lead to orgasm is an important realization.

Sweet, Sweet Porn

I talked briefly about porn earlier in this chapter. It is a very loaded topic. I was having a very intimate conversation with my friend Kevin the other day when the topic turned to porn:

"She says it is like having an emotional affair." Kevin was almost incredulous that his wife could feel that way.

"Well, let me ask you. When you are upset at her or you guys are fighting, do you go to the porn instead of her?" I asked, hoping I might be able to help him explore this issue without feeling attacked or judged.

"Well, yeah."

"And when you feel rejected or abandoned by her, do you go to the porn?"

"Well, yeah. And she told me to stop watching it because she said it was like me cheating on her, so I said I would stop. "

"And you didn't, right?"

"Right. Who is she to tell me what to do?"

"Okay, so that becomes an excuse for you to lie to her in your marriage? And you wonder how she could say it is like having an emotional affair?"

Imagine you are a man like Kevin and you have just had a fight with your partner. Your feelings are hurt. It hits a wound inside you from the past. You may or may not realize this. With the wound hurting, you run straight into the arms of your lover. If you're in recovery, this used to be alcohol and/or other drugs. Now, you go into the basement and turn on your computer, or go to the closest strip joint, or maybe a massage parlor. Porn will never turn you away. Porn does not require any intimacy. Porn does not demand your vulnerability or accountability for your behavior, or for you to even communicate. You don't need to stop and listen or acknowledge the other being who is part of the relationship.

Maybe you are a man who finds it difficult to talk about sex with his partner. You do not know how to ask for what you want. That was a very common response from the men I interviewed when I asked how comfortable they felt talking to their partners about sex. Mark said he was "moderately comfortable and improving. It is easy to ask for attention and difficult to say specifically what I need." If you have sexual abuse in your history, it could be even more difficult. There are many other scenarios I could describe that can drive men toward using pornography: You're new to recovery and don't know how to talk to women or men; you were wounded as a child sexually and have never been able to be open about sex or your sexuality with another; you're simply curious; you're looking for something to enhance your sex life (there are couples who use porn as a way to enhance their relationship); or your partner doesn't want to have sex as much as you do. Regardless of the reason, if porn is a secret in your relationship, it is a problem.

There is nothing wrong with masturbation in and of itself. It plays many important roles in a man's sexuality. It can help to relieve stress, it helps men to get to know their bodies and to explore their sexuality, it takes care of our sexual desires without putting demands on our partner, and there is some evidence from research in Europe that says that men who masturbate and achieve orgasm at least four times a week greatly reduce the risk of prostate cancer. In early recovery, masturbation can be an important outlet for some men to keep them from acting out with others newly in recovery and vulnerable to the seduction of quick connections. When I first got into recovery, my sponsor, Bill, told me the three M's would help me make it through: Meetings, Meditation, and Masturbation. However, for some men in sexual recovery, the practice of *not* masturbating is part of their recovery program. This is your journey— be thoughtful, talk to others, and honor what is important to you.

Body Image

Every man I know has some sort of struggle with body image. Today, in the media, men are assailed with reasons to feel less than and insecure about our bodies as much as women. But it takes a strong man to talk about this.

As I've described, one of the toughest issues I have dealt with in my life, let alone my most intimate relationships, has been around body image and being treated with shots of testosterone to induce puberty. That process burned into my consciousness the inherent deficiency of my body, my brokenness as a man, and my defective sexuality and led to such deep trauma that I still sometimes struggle to see myself as a man in a man's body. If you were to look at me, you would never know that. There is so much that we cannot see or know about other men by their appearance alone.

Often I still can see that scrawny prepubescent kid looking back at me in the mirror. He haunted me for twenty-five years. I know today it is called "body dysmorphia," and it's a form of the body image distortion that people with anorexia and bulimia frequently struggle with. Long into my recovery and my marriage, I struggled immensely with body image. Nancy could never understand until I sat her down and explained to her with tears in my eyes, at forty-one years old and with nineteen years in recovery, how incredibly difficult this has been for me.

Nancy knew her own struggles with body image. Like a lot of people, she didn't even think of men as having body image issues, and certainly could not imagine how I could have them because she made the mistake we make with men all the time: She was only looking at my body and not listening to me. What I've learned is that, contrary to popular belief, the majority of men struggle with some kind of body image issue because our bodies—and how strong we are, how tall we are, how muscular we are, our growing old and losing muscle mass and strength, how well-endowed we are, and so forth—are deeply connected to how we feel about ourselves as men.

After I opened up about my body image challenges at the men's retreat, every single one of the men talked about how my work on this area of my life resonated with them. Some of them said that they had had similar experiences and had never talked about it, or even thought about it, their whole life until that day. This experience taught me that there are a lot of men who are hurting in similar ways. In fact, every time I travel and speak about this, there are inevitably men who come up to me and talk to me about their experience, sometimes for the first time. Even if a man is "blessed" with being good-looking, tall, strong, and athletic, you never know what struggles he may have.

Let's not avoid the most sensitive area of men's body image: the penis. The great symbol of masculinity and strength, or so we are led to believe. If you were to do a contextual analysis, you would see that in the past ten years the number of references to a man's penis in movies and shows, along with the suggestions that if he is not well-endowed he is less of a man and if he is well-endowed his "man card" is confirmed for perpetuity, has skyrocketed. Some women might say, "Well, now you know how it feels. We have been judged by our bodies and beauty for decades in the media. It is only fair that you experience the same opportunities for shame and self-disgust." There is some real truth to that. But it doesn't make it any less sad or tragic. It is no coincidence that body image, which I purposely did not ask about in my interviews for this book, only came up once, from Nate when asked about his comfort in talking about sex with his partner: "I can talk to her about sex and other topics but have had a hard time letting her know about my insecurities regarding body image and desirability." For how many men is the essence of that statement true?

Sex, Intimacy, and Love

If you are one of those guys who spends a lot of time complaining about how little sex you get from your partner, I can guarantee you it is not just about them. In that circumstance, chances are the biggest challenge is for both partners to have an open, honest, and vulnerable conversation about their sexual desires, needs, and fears.

For those of us who have struggled with addiction, we are often disconnected from life and disconnected from our bodies. That makes it difficult to experience our sexuality as something other than the act of sex. It certainly was difficult for me. With enough liquid courage, I could talk to women. With enough luck, they would be interested in me. Then it was game on. And it was a game, because it was all about winning and getting what I wanted so that I could briefly feel better about myself, with little to no real regard for the other person. Jim talked about this mentality both before and after getting into recovery: "Prior to recovery, sexuality was all about power and conquest. I was a man because I had sex with lots of people. Some of this continues in recovery, outwardly. I find there is still a great deal of posturing about sex and sex experiences—who has had sex with more people, who is more macho. Having the biggest dick means you are the biggest man type of thing."

I was scared to death of intimacy. I had no idea what it was, but I wanted it. We all did. That was why we would find ourselves having deep conversations despite our slurred speech. That was why we would scope each other out at parties to find someone with whom we could connect. I found myself talking to prospective partners for the night about my home life, my challenges with school, my hopes and dreams. I did not see it as manipulative, but I always had an agenda. However, I also needed to share it with someone so that I could feel a little more real. Without alcohol or some other substance, though, I was just the shadow of a man.

I wanted love, but my heart had hardened. I had no idea how much so, but twenty years of recovery have not completely healed the wounds. We have an innate human desire for love—to love and to be loved. How many times did I fall in love in college? Sometimes I'd fall in love for the night. Sometimes it was an unrequited love where I did not even have the courage to talk to the woman. But the desire for it was always there. Using sex as the sole support to meet the need for intimacy and love doesn't work. It didn't work for me, and I do not believe it works for anyone.

My experience is that sex, intimacy, and love are separate phenomena that, when brought together, are amazing. That is a big part of what my sexuality is. I describe it as having spent my life eating McDonald's hamburgers and thinking they were filet mignon. Until I actually had filet mignon, in other words, until I experienced sex in the space of love and intimacy, I had no idea how good it could be. Until I experienced love in a relationship where sex and intimacy accentuate a connection unlike anything I have ever known, I had no idea how good it could be. Guy talked about this when he said, "Sex is now not the number-one priority. Great sex is the culmination rather than the beginning of the relationship." Your sexuality, each and every component of it, can be whatever works best for you. There are no rules as long as it does not harm others.

It can take a lot of time and effort to create the synergy that occurs when sex, love, and intimacy combine, but it is well worth it. And until you have experienced it, you really have no idea what you are missing. Larry summed up the process of developing a healthy sex life beautifully: "Safety, then intimacy, then sex."

Into Action

► Please answer the following questions in your notebook:
  • What do I think sex is for?
  • How do I use my sexuality in a healthy way?
  • How do I use my sexuality in an unhealthy way?
  • How have I harmed others sexually?

► Take some time right now to think about how the sex funnel shows up in your life.
  • What happens to you when you experience affection for another man?
  • What happens when you connect in conversation with an attractive woman or man (depending on your sexual orientation)?

► Set up a time to talk to your partner about your sex life. Be clear about what you want to discuss. Ask them ahead of time to write down answers to the following questions. You do the same.
  • What do you like the most?
  • What would you like to be different?
  • What would you like to try sexually that you have never tried?
  • On a scale of one to ten, one being completely dissatisfied, how satisfactory is the frequency of sex?
  • What scares you the most about sex?
  • What else do you need to feel satisfied with your sex life?

► What is your relationship to pornography? Answer the following questions:
  • How old were you when you saw your first pornography?
  • How often do you use pornography now?
  • What is happening in your relationship when you turn to porn?
  • What does your partner know about your use of porn? If they do not know, why not?
  • What is your experience with erotica versus pornography?

Advanced Into Action

► When you are with your partner and you get sexually aroused, make a conscious decision not to engage in sex.

► Ask your partner to hold you when you feel scared, insecure, or sad, and don't have it turn to sex.

CHAPTER ELEVEN
Separating the Men from the Boys

"I see myself integrating all of my selves:
boy, teen, man, creative." –Luke

If every chapter is a part of the map that we have been delineating, then this chapter is the subterranean part. These are the forces that are far beneath the surface that are very difficult to see. There is an irony to the title of this chapter as it relates to us men creating healthy relationships in our recovery. A common belief in recovery is that we have to leave behind all that is a boy in us so that we can be mature men. We have to "grow the 'F' up!" as I once heard in a men's retreat. That is true to an extent. There is no question that when we first get into recovery a lot of us are nothing more than little boys, particularly when it comes to our relationships. But the clarion call to "grow up" often becomes a way for men to beat their inner little kid into submission. That may work in the short run, but never in the long run.

Interestingly, as you mature and grow in recovery you realize that becoming a mature and healthy man includes learning how, as Luke said in the quote above, to integrate the boy and the adolescent into your adult self. Part of this process involves learning to accept our childhood.

As I've described, getting to the place where I could accept my childhood took many years and a great deal of work. Many men would much rather forget their childhood than accept it. A lot of us couldn't wait to be done with that little boy because he was everything the Rules tell us a man isn't: small, weak, emotional, sensitive, and powerless. For a lot of us, adolescence was a painful time when we experienced the trade-off of turning our backs on our humanity so we could be seen as something closer to men. Even for those of us who rejected the stereotypes of masculinity, chances are adolescence was a painful process of letting go of childhood, walking reluctantly into adulthood, and stumbling into manhood.

Like a lot of men, I have a very strong adolescent energy. There is nothing wrong with that, but when it is making decisions and determining my behavior, the results aren't pretty. That young man has gotten me fired from almost every job I ever had and put me in conflict with almost every authority figure who has ever crossed my path. The same thing goes with the scared little boy. When we make peace with him, we make peace with both of them. If this sounds like B.S. to you, I know the feeling. I carried very strong and reactive judgments about these ideas with me for many years of my recovery. Your reaction might just be the exact reason why you need to look at them. That was the case for me. I kept running into people who suggested I connect with that wounded child. It always sounded so silly. But then I met Earnie Larsen.

Earnie suggested that I try to love that child who wasn't loved the way he needed to be. Just hearing him say that, I felt myself want to throw up. I had been around men's work where they did inner child work, and it all seemed so absurd. Having men regress into a little child, even to the point of acting like a baby? Really? The truth is that different approaches work for different people, but the question I had to ask myself was, *Why do I have such a strong reaction to these ideas?* I would hear grown men talk about their inner child, and I would have an overwhelming desire to ridicule them or punch them in the face. It was a visceral disgust. You don't have to be a brilliant therapist to figure out that that reaction was out of proportion to something that is just an idea. Clearly, this idea touched my internal wounds.

For a long time I fought the idea of the "inner child" because it seems so unmanly. Little boys are not men; quite the opposite: They represent a lot of what is not manly. Why would I want to make peace with him? I just wanted him out of the way so I could get on with the business of struggling to become a man and someday hopefully being able to see myself as a man. I never realized that if I could not make peace with that little boy I would never feel like a man, because that wounded part of myself would continue to run the show of my life.

I learned from Earnie and his wife, Paula, that it could be a simple exercise like imagining putting that child on my lap every morning and letting him know that he is safe and I love him and am going to take care of him. I came up with something perfect for me that I could wrap my hypercritical mind around. I loved football when I was a kid and was great at it. Unfortunately, my mom would not let me play because she didn't want me to get hurt. Every once in a while I could get my father to throw the football with me, but those times were few and far between and always included some kind of criticism or derision. Looking back, I can see that he was so critical of me because he was so critical of himself. Now, on a regular basis I imagine myself throwing the football with my little seven-year-old self and my teenage self. That has helped me to feel more peaceful not only about those parts of myself, but also about my father and even my mother. As the wounds heal, I get to free my parents from the blame that I have been carrying.

Big-Boy Pants

You will probably hear this saying in a men's recovery meeting if you attend long enough: "It's time to put on your big-boy pants." Personally, I love that saying. It's another way of saying, "Grow up and stop acting like a child." You are a big boy with big-boy responsibilities, so it is time for you to start acting like it. With a caution, however.

The reality is that as adults we should always have our big-boy pants on. The challenge for every man is in how he balances being an adult with taking care of his wounded internal child. Does he take his metaphorical Underoos and throw them away? Rip them off and castigate the little boy who was wearing them? No, it means saying, "I am going to take care of myself and others I am responsible for, and that includes you."

The other part of putting our big-boy pants on is to not let that prevent us from embracing that wonderful childlike energy inside us. Keeping in contact with this energy is a way not only of mitigating pain, but also of rediscovering joy, which is so important to recovery. It is the innocent child in us who can be transfixed by a new idea, image, or activity. It is the child who is open to wonder and mystery and having fun. Children simply are. They put their effort into expressing their needs, not trying to hide them. So, we don't have to simply make peace with our inner child; we should reawaken him and just make sure that we watch over him and play the parent when we need to.

The Roles in Addicted Families

A classic typology in the addictions field developed by Sharon Wegscheider-Cruse and Claudia Black describes the different roles people take on in families where addiction is present. Every family has roles similar to these, but the more dysfunctional the family is, the more rigid and calcified these roles tend to become. In addicted family systems, the children are there to meet the needs of the parents and to keep the addiction from being addressed. The roles are:

The Chief Enabler/Codependent is the other "head" of the household who spends most of his or her time cleaning up the messes of the addict and protecting him or her from the consequences of his or her behavior.

The Hero is the child who overachieves. The Hero takes it upon him- or herself to be the perfect child and project to the world that everything is "fine" in the family. A great deal of pressure is put on them (including by themselves) to succeed and look good as the public face of the family.

The Scapegoat is the classic troublemaker; sadly, this poor young person assumes the burden of the chaos in the family system by acting out and drawing attention away from the addiction. The assumption is that the problem is not the family, it's the scapegoat! Get that little ne'er-do-well under control and everything will be fine.

The Invisible Child is the one who stays in his or her room by him- or herself, reading, watching TV, or playing video games to the point where he or she is almost forgotten. The Invisible Child does not make waves; his or her pain is silent and internalized.

The Mascot is the joker who helps to defuse the incredible tension in the family by being cute and joking around. If people are laughing, it makes difficult circumstances more bearable. But inside, the Mascot cries the tears of the clown.

The way these roles are listed here tends to correspond with birth order, but it varies from one family to another and varies according to the size of the family. For instance, as one of two children I took on the roles of Scapegoat and Mascot. The most important part of understanding your role as an adult is seeing how it still shows up—in your family of origin, your current family, your workplace, and other group situations.

Adult Children of Addiction

Adult Children of Alcoholics (ACA) is another twelve-step program started by men in recovery who realized that they were experiencing challenges that didn't seem to have anything to do with their addiction. They found themselves struggling with their relationships in profound ways, and something seemed to be missing in their healing.

One of the guiding principles of ACA is the idea that we become the loving parent to ourselves we wish we had growing up. That is such a powerful concept. It means that, once and for all, we take off the scarlet "V for victim" hanging around our neck. Our parents and primary caregivers are not to blame for our lives and how they have turned out. This does not mean that what they did was okay or should be forgotten. What it does mean is that we are not children anymore and it is our responsibility to do the work to make peace with our childhood, our parents, and our perceptions of what happened to us as children. Nick talked about this process and noted the generational transmission of trauma when he said, "I have therapeutically released most of my anger toward my parents and I can see how their parents were absolutely terrible. I have fewer or almost no resentments at their poor parenting choices as a result."

When we do this work, we make peace with the inner victim who drives so much of our lives. Where did that victim come from? It most often comes out of the victimization that someone has had to endure, very often as a child. It is the wounded part of who we are that never healed. Healing requires learning how to have compassion for the inner victim and to be gentle with the part of ourselves that feels so wounded.

In 2013 I was invited to be one of the main speakers for a wonderful conference in Florida that brings people in AA, Al-Anon, and ACA all together at the same time. This conference is an amazing opportunity for people in recovery from addiction to alcohol and other drugs, as well as those who have been deeply affected by the addiction of others, to come together and be exposed to different aspects of recovery. What was so special and powerful for me was that it was the first time I was able to tell my whole story without feeling as though I needed to hold back any part of it.

My story of recovery started when I attended a workshop at my college, looking at growing up in an alcoholic family. For the first time I heard other people talking about the pain of living in the insanity of watching someone you love and hate slowly drink himself to death. It was a couple of months into that process when Randy, from this book, who was my counselor, looked at me and said, "I think you've got it" (addiction). That first ACA group and the people in it changed my life forever. I found the first place in my life where I could bring my pain and no one laughed at me. I felt safer there than I had felt anywhere for a very long time. The only challenge was that I was the only man in the group, so it reinforced the belief that I did not really fit in with other men.

Early in my recovery, what that conference in Florida helped me remember was how powerful the effects of growing up in a violent alcoholic home were on my life and my relationships. When Nancy first read *Struggle for Intimacy,* a classic book about the challenges ACAs have in forming relationships, it gave her a whole new level of understanding of why relationships were so hard for me. It helped her to better understand where some of my behaviors were coming from. I told her I loved her, and yet I treated her like the enemy sometimes. I was so sensitive to anything she said that could be perceived or misperceived as criticism. I was in recovery and working in a professional job, yet seemed quite immature. I had a lot of the characteristics noted on the ACA Laundry List and Nancy could not understand it because at times I presented so well. I wasn't an impostor; I simply was someone who, in the face of increased intimacy and stress, didn't know how to navigate the intense feelings I was experiencing.

When any of my childhood wounds was triggered, I would feel like a child. The shame was overwhelming. It happens a lot less since I have done a lot of the healing work. I notice when it is happening. I notice when I might be vulnerable for it to happen. If I slip into a full-on trauma relapse, I feel fear, shame, insecurity, powerlessness, and other very uncomfortable and unmanly feelings all at the same time. I have slipped into the limbic part of my brain and am unable to process the experience in the context of the current moment. Instead, I am that scared and abandoned child—again.

The Laundry List

The Laundry List was the first piece of ACA literature. It is a list of fourteen characteristics or traits common to adult children of alcoholics/ addicts. These hit home for so many people in recovery primarily because so many of us come from highly chaotic, if not addicted, family systems that deeply affected us as children. Yet we often do not see them—they were so "normal" for us that they simply became more of the Water in which we swim.

(Note: The ACA Laundry List is Copyrighted by Adult Children of Alcoholics World Service Organization and is reprinted with permission of Adult Children of Alcoholic/Dysfunctional Families World Services, Inc. There is no affiliation between ACA and the author or the author's views.)

The Laundry List—14 Traits of an Adult Child of an Alcoholic

1. We became isolated and afraid of people and authority figures.
2. We became approval seekers and lost our identity in the process.
3. We are frightened by angry people and any personal criticism.
4. We either become alcoholics, marry them, or both, or find another compulsive personality such as a workaholic to fulfill our sick abandonment needs.
5. We live life from the viewpoint of victims and we are attracted by that weakness in our love and friendship relationships.
6. We have an overdeveloped sense of responsibility and it is easier for us to be concerned with others rather than ourselves; this enables us not to look too closely at our own faults, etc.
7. We get guilt feelings when we stand up for ourselves instead of giving in to others.
8. We become addicted to excitement.
9. We confuse love and pity and tend to "love" people we can "pity" and "rescue."
10. We have "stuffed" our feelings from our traumatic childhoods and have lost the ability to feel or express our feelings because it hurts so much (denial).
11. We judge ourselves harshly and have a very low sense of self-esteem.
12. We are dependent personalities who are terrified of abandonment and will do anything to hold on to a relationship in order not to experience painful abandonment feelings, which we received from living with sick people who were never there emotionally for us.
13. Alcoholism is a family disease; and we became para-alcoholics and took on the characteristics of that disease even though we did not pick up the drink.
14. Para-alcoholics are reactors rather than actors.

I will discuss each of these traits briefly.

We became isolated and afraid of people and authority figures.
It was horrible how much time I spent in my jobs afraid of my boss
and coworkers, or anyone with perceived power. Like a lot of men, my
fear presented as disrespect, anger, and defiance, but it was fear, pure and
simple.

We became approval seekers and lost our identity in the process.
"Please like me!" Many of the men I interviewed talked about their deep
need to be liked and accepted, often at the expense of their peace of
mind and/or dignity.

We are frightened by angry people and any personal criticism.
If you grew up in a home with violence and abuse, you know that
expressed anger was often a sign of worse things to come. When we
encounter angry people as adults, those memories and past fears are
triggered. Also, if you think you are a piece of shit because that is what
you were told growing up, you will continue to believe that about
yourself.

**We either become alcoholics, marry them or both, or find
another compulsive personality such as a workaholic to fulfill
our sick abandonment needs.** Our emotional abandonment needs
create a vacuum. That vacuum will be filled, usually with that which is
familiar to us, and it is amazing how hard it is for us to see this.

**We live life from the viewpoint of victims and we are attracted
by that weakness in our love and friendship relationships.**
Many men don't want to admit how often we act like victims, or that
we victimize others. We may hide it with our pseudo-adult persona
and our macho posturing, but it exerts considerable influence on our
relationships.

**We have an overdeveloped sense of responsibility and it is easier
for us to be concerned with others rather than ourselves; this**

enables us not to look too closely at our own faults, etc. This was not a major issue for me until I started to have some success as a professional and started my own business. It is especially common for people who played the role of Hero in their family system. Focusing on others is always easier than looking at ourselves. But it is not just the Hero who is susceptible to this experience. For many of us, in moving into adult responsibilities we run into feelings of fear and shame that we mask with perfectionism and hyperresponsibility.

We get guilt feelings when we stand up for ourselves instead of giving in to others. For the first five years or so of my recovery I didn't stand up, I blew up. I would stuff and stuff and finally my top would blow—usually toward those I perceived to be weaker than me. I have never been a doormat, but I had a really hard time standing up for myself in a healthy way. This can still be a tough one for me. The hardest part is the guilt that comes when we do stand up for ourselves, even if it is in a healthy way. Are they mad at me? Did I ruin the relationship? Am I just being an asshole or petty? I would second-guess myself many times when I attempted to deal with conflict.

We became addicted to excitement. Addicted family systems thrive on chaos. Our brains and bodies get wired for excitement—literally. When things are calm, we don't know what is coming, or when. In addicted families, what *could* be coming next is always scariest. This is one of the reasons quiet relaxation and meditation in adulthood can be so uncomfortable, and so important to our healing.

We confuse love and pity and tend to "love" people we can "pity" and "rescue." A lot of men, especially male addicts, find ACA women (and men) who will pity and rescue us. We find friends and partners with codependent traits and behavior. But there are also many men who find themselves trying to rescue or save someone and feeling miserable because they are unable to do so.

We have "stuffed" our feelings from our traumatic childhoods and have lost the ability to feel or express our feelings because it hurts so much (denial). Men can talk about how we are feeling, but actually feeling it is a lot harder because it makes us vulnerable and can leave us feeling weak and exposed.

We judge ourselves harshly and have a very low sense of self-esteem. It is amazing how many of the men I interviewed struggled with such a deep sense of self-criticism, even self-loathing. Behind the hyperconfidence or the constant smiles and "Mr. Happy" exterior is a highly self-critical part of themselves that they struggle to shake.

We are dependent personalities who are terrified of abandonment and will do anything to hold onto a relationship in order not to experience painful abandonment feelings, which we received from living with sick people who were never there emotionally for us. I have watched this happen over and over again in my life. It is amazing how many men in recovery choose partners (despite the stereotype of men as emotionally unavailable) who are emotionally unavailable. It is a volatile mix because we crave connection and love, and if we do not get it we feel abandoned and then we act out—setting our partner up to pull away more.

Alcoholism is a family disease; and we became para-alcoholics and took on the characteristics of that disease even though we did not pick up the drink. Obviously a lot of us did in fact pick up that first drink, joint, pipe, or needle (or whatever). The point is that once we stop using alcohol and other drugs, the other characteristics of the disease of addiction don't just go away. That's where the Twelve Steps and other sources of support come in.

Para-alcoholics are reactors rather than actors. We go through life being thrown around by it rather than considering how we want to act. Even when we do pause to think about how we want to respond, in the face of stress or high emotion—when we slip into the limbic system in our brain—we react impulsively. The more healing work we do, the more the power of choice is restored in our lives.

What does it mean for me to say as a grown man that I struggle with the pain from childhood? There is a macho posturing that keeps men in their pain: *"What, are you going to cry about your sad childhood?" "Are you going to whine because Daddy didn't love you enough?"* Or perhaps there are the less obnoxious reactions, such as *"There is no use spending time in the past; live in the present."* The core message is the same: *"Get over it!"* Sometimes these comments are well-meaning, made as they are by men who have seen so many men stay in "victim" mode in their attempts to heal. They know how crippling and self-defeating that can be. Other times it is men speaking from the depths of their own wounds and the trauma they have not yet healed from. They are afraid to acknowledge that pain themselves, so they shame others. There is no question that we are a traumatized community of men trying our very best to create healthy and fulfilling lives. For many of these men, at the heart of their suffering is the unresolved pain from their childhood. Many of us remain wounded children who are still searching for peace.

There is nothing like having children to help us make peace with our own childhood. I have found that Grace has given me incredible opportunities to reconnect with my childhood. If I am not paying attention, I react to her through the eyes of that wounded child, losing compassion for her and judging her harshly when her only crime is acting like the four-year-old she is—a crazy little four-year-old trying to make sense of her world and all of the little wants and needs inside her that she has such a limited awareness of.

However, you don't have to have children or be in recovery to do this work or to heal. Maybe you have a niece or nephew, or a "little brother" through the YMCA. Maybe you do this work with the aid of your pets. At some point we have a decision to make: Are we going to become fully integrated human beings, or are we going to continue to live fragmented lives?

Every time I would try to be more honest about my experiences growing up, I would immediately be assaulted by the voice saying,

"Don't be such a _____ (fill in the expletive)." I struggled so desperately to have compassion for myself and the little boy who had experienced so much pain growing up. I couldn't get past the harsh judgments that I was just being weak and exaggerating what happened to me. That abrasive self-judgment lies at the heart of many men's abuse—it was *your* fault. Let me be perfectly clear: It is not true.

No matter what you did or what anyone said, *it was not your fault*. It is impossible for a child to do anything that would cause the people who are supposed to love and protect him to betray him by abdicating their responsibility as parents and as caregivers. Yet, how many MILLIONS of boys grew up with this experience? How many men are still haunted by it? We hear it in our homes. Then it is repeated at the schools, then in the service delivery systems, then in the criminal justice system. Even the addictions field has a degree of it—especially directed toward men. The underlying message: There is something wrong with you. We have to continue to talk about this lie and create a space for men to heal from the wounds that are not only hurting them but eating away at every relationship they have. We deserve better, and so do those who so much want to love us.

There is a saying that it's never too late to have a happy childhood. When I first heard that line, it gave me hope. Is it true? It is if you decide it to be. My childhood has been transformed as a result of the work I have done in recovery. I have been able to look at it through new eyes. The experiences haven't changed. But the bad has become less bad. And the good has become much better. I am learning how to live with it and accept it—all of it.

Into Action

- ▶ Find a book on adult children (listed in Additional Resources) and take the time to read it.

- ▶ Find a local ACA meeting (you can visit www.adultchildren.org).

- ▶ Take some time and review the Laundry List included in this chapter. Look at each item, and if you identify with it write three examples of how and three things that you can do to help yourself address the impact of that specific list item.

- ▶ Ask your partner to review the Laundry List and see what items they think apply to you and compare those to the ones you think fit for you. Have a discussion about this.

- ▶ Write a letter to one or both of your parents (not to send) in which you can express anything you need to about your experiences growing up. It can run the gamut of anger, gratitude, hatred, sadness, grief, and confusion—all of it is okay.

CHAPTER TWELVE
Codependency

*"It's the underlying first addiction. Al-Anon is
the graduate school for AA." —Sean*

Let's get one thing straight right now: Men with and without addiction and in recovery not only experience the codependence of others, especially the women in their lives, but they can also exhibit codependent behaviors themselves. Because of the classic image of the male addict paired with a female codependent, codependency is generally associated with women. In spite of the reality that men can be codependent to both women and men and both men and women can be codependent to their children, many men still view codependence as feminine and believe that to say they have codependent behaviors means something about them as men. Ed talked about this: "I may see issues less through the prism of gender than other men. I sense some of my male peers see codependency as a female issue." That is an ill-informed and fairly naïve perspective.

Did you ever find yourself agreeing to do something with someone and really not wanting to do it or even to be with him or her? Or maybe you agreed to go to a specific place with him or her when you really wanted to go somewhere else. Codependency occurs when we chronically neglect our own desires and needs for the sake of approval and/or in a covert attempt to exert some sort of control over others.

Codependency exists when we need everyone else to follow our agenda or we have to follow someone else's agenda in order to feel okay. Codependency blurs the appropriate boundaries between people and doesn't allow for the possibility that each of us has unique and different paths that are of equal merit and value. Being in a relationship doesn't mean that both parties have to follow the exact same path at all times; it means that we commit to being connected with each other, respecting each other's journey, and making sure that our paths cross often.

First, let's define codependency, because there is often a lot of confusion around what it is and what it is not. For the purposes of this discussion, the definition of codependency I am using is a simple one: a pattern of destructive and/or self-destructive behaviors focused on changing or controlling another's behavior that interfere with a man's ability to care for himself and set healthy boundaries with others. It is important to know that at times every man exhibits some codependent behaviors in his relationships. Emilio talked about the danger of labeling people as codependent: "I understand that I exhibit some of these behaviors and have some awareness there, but some of these are natural behaviors of fathers and husbands. I have to care enough to let others find their way, and yet still reach out my hand to help in healthy ways." Emilio is saying that if you care about and love someone, there will always be a gray area where the line between codependent behavior and simply caring deeply about or loving someone and doing it imperfectly can be unclear.

Larry made an excellent point: "I'm not sure I believe in the concept of codependency. I think it's our natural state to be in relationships. That said, there are obviously healthy and not-so-healthy relationships." The term *codependent* has become overused and can be a way of unfairly judging people's natural struggle to find balance in their relationships with others.

When we begin to see a pattern of behavior related to how we care about others that has consistent negative impacts on our quality of life, then there is a problem. When that pattern of behavior leads to problems in different life areas and creates mental and emotional distress, we move into the realm of an actual disorder for which we need help to change learned patterns of thinking and relating to others. Often, at the heart of these problematic patterns we find trauma, particularly from childhood, where we learned unhealthy ways of relating to others by virtue of the tangled web of dysfunctional relationships we were trapped in. At the heart of these relationship difficulties are problems developing secure attachment in intimate relationships—the more intimate the relationship, the greater the challenges of healthy attachment. Research has consistently shown that there really are no gender differences in how boys and girls experience the challenges of compromised and inconsistent attachment.

Here are just some of the common scenarios that reflect men's struggle with codependent thoughts and behaviors. You will probably identify with at least one of these scenarios, although you may not see them as codependent:

- A man wants to please—or not hurt—his partner, so he puts up with inappropriate, unacceptable, and even abusive behavior.
- A man has a hard time saying no to people because he is worried about them getting upset at him or not liking him. However, he is often resentful about this, even though he feels guilty at the thought of taking care of himself and saying no.
- A man stays in a relationship that he is not emotionally invested in because it is too scary for him to have a more meaningful relationship or to be alone.
- A man is afraid to set boundaries with his boss or colleagues because he is worried about them not liking him or getting upset at him if he does.
- A man attempts to control the behavior of his spouse and/ or his children because he is afraid of what might happen to them and is unable to communicate his fear, so it comes out as controlling and angry, particularly when they do not act as he expects them to.
- A man is afraid to ask for what he really needs and to express his hurt feelings in his most intimate relationships because he is worried that he will not be seen as a strong man to those he loves most.
- A man says "yes" when he means "no"; he laughs when something really isn't funny; he does things he doesn't want to

do so he can fit in and says things he knows don't reflect what he believes, but is afraid to speak up for himself.

Just because you identify with one or all of these examples doesn't mean you are a codependent in need of treatment. These are simply flags pointing toward a problematic tendency to please others and take care of them while neglecting your own needs. You may also be wondering how I came up with these examples. Well, I took them all from my own life and experience in relationships. Every single one of them has been an issue at some point in my life, including as recently as yesterday. Do any of these scenarios seem familiar to you? Don't let your potential bias against the idea of codependency prevent you from looking at the dissatisfaction and pain these kinds of thoughts and behaviors may be causing in your life. If you find a consistent pattern, it could be to your benefit to look at them more intentionally by attending Al-Anon meetings, working with a therapist, or attending workshops or professional programs specifically designed to help men look at codependent tendencies.

That *Other* Fellowship

Many of the men I interviewed talked about their attendance in Al-Anon. Several of the men joked that the only time they stopped going was when they got into a relationship! Of course, the humorous part about it is that that would have been the time they needed it the most. It is amazing to me how many men still dismiss or mock Al-Anon because it has traditionally been for women. Earlier in my recovery someone told me that Al-Anon is advanced AA. This makes sense to me, because the focus is so much on relationships and learning how to be emotionally healthy and detached in relationships. We move away from the other person, and the focus is on getting well ourselves rather than on fixing the relationship. Think about what Sean said at the beginning of this chapter: "It's the underlying first addiction. Al-Anon is the graduate school for AA." At the heart of it, Al-Anon builds relational competency by improving emotional awareness and one's ability to set healthy boundaries.

According to Al-Anon World Services, a growing demographic in Al-Anon is the men. Al-Anon is the twelve-step program for the significant others and family members of alcoholics. There are a number of men whose sole form of addiction is their "addiction" to the *person* with whom they are in relationship. I have sat with those men and watched the pain they experienced as they continued to love their partner amid the chaos and confusion created by their partner's active addiction. The truth is, I have never met a man, whether in recovery or not, who couldn't benefit from looking a little more deeply into the idea of codependency by attending a few meetings with a therapist or support group of some kind.

There is a saying in twelve-step programs that addicts don't get into relationships; they take hostages. While this saying is usually intended to be humorous, most everyone who hears it understands its serious side. Our closest relationships are the ones in which we express our most unhealthy behaviors, usually as a way of protecting our vulnerability and hiding our shame. The question for men is whether we are man enough to admit that we struggle with issues of codependency too. Over and over again I have watched men with ten, twenty, and thirty years in recovery begin to see that underlying their biggest relationship challenges is a struggle to be vulnerable; to know, let alone ask for, what they need; and to be able to set healthy boundaries with others to take better care of themselves.

Male Codependence, Anger, and Aggression

(This section comes specifically from concepts developed with my training partner and colleague, Rick Dauer.)

A question that Rick and I have sought to address is whether or not the common definitions and books on codependency really speak to men's experience with the issue. Would it surprise you if I said that a lot of the abuse that men commit comes out of our struggles with codependence? How is that? One of the Man Rules is that men aren't allowed to experience any emotion other than anger in some form. Using the concept of the anger funnel discussed earlier, often underneath men's anger are the more vulnerable emotions of hurt, sadness, insecurity, fear, and so on. Believe it or not, many men avoid conflict, put up with inappropriate or abusive behavior at work and/or at home, and shut down emotionally by either isolating, doing their own thing, or people-pleasing. Something has got to give. We either implode or explode if we do not deal with the challenges causing us discomfort and pain.

Rick and I believe that a lot of men's anger hides their codependency. For instance, every time I have yelled at or been mean to someone, at some level it has been connected to my challenges with codependent behavior. Sometimes it is me being unable to detach enough from their behavior and what I think I know about their intentions. I am being overly sensitive. Or, I feel like they are putting me down or criticizing me, and I let that often incorrect perception carry too much weight. Other times it is my lack of a strong enough sense of who I am, separate from anything the other person says or does. My personal struggles with this issue have been chronic, persistent, and debilitating at times. It has gotten so much better, but for so long the traits of the ACA Laundry List ruled my life. I credit my progress to my willingness to be vulnerable (much more than I wanted to be) on a regular basis with those to whom I am closest, despite my regular and somewhat constant failures in being the man I truly wanted to be.

If you think about it, most of the traits of codependency I just described seem to be at odds with the Man Rules. Traits such as insecurity, neediness, enmeshment, passivity, and putting up with abusive and inappropriate behavior all scream of weakness; they are unmanly. The truth is that men who struggle with shame, who lack the ability to navigate their relationships in healthy ways (which we come by honestly through our upbringing), and who aren't able to identify and/or communicate what they feel have two basic choices: express the above traits—which are all signs of weakness and exacerbate the shame of not feeling like a man—or isolate, shut down, or act aggressively, which pushes others away. At some level we think our masculinity is intact despite the damage we have done to our relationships. What a double bind!

There are a great many men who, when they have drilled down beneath their anger, workaholism, isolation, and need for control, discover codependence. They see how much pressure they put on themselves to be perfect, to have all the answers, and to fix whatever problems their partner, boss, or friends are having. Jose talked about this: "My struggle has been wanting to be everything to everyone sometimes and falling short. Falling short results in me being resentful at them and myself." Almost every single man I interviewed, particularly those in recovery for quite some time and/or who have done intensive men's work or trauma work, is clear that his relationships are full of codependent behaviors and hiding behind the Man Rules. The more honest they get about the feelings underlying many of their behaviors, the more they see codependency.

Marty said that "seeing codependent behavior in myself is bothersome to me, as I view it as a weakness." That statement is exactly what keeps so many of us men from looking honestly at our codependent behaviors. Luke said, "I struggle with wanting to save or fix other people I care about. There are times that I judge myself to be less than a man when I can't control what others do/don't do or say/don't say."

Allen Berger talks about the idea of "holding onto yourself" in relationships. This concept speaks to the importance of carrying our whole selves into our relationships and holding onto our whole selves in our relationships. Of course, this is a fluctuating experience. Sometimes we do it better than others. This is more of a struggle for men than we like to admit. Mike talked about how he has come to see his challenges with codependent behavior as being "the trade-off between my need to control (destructive) and standing strong for myself as a man; between having to have it 'my way' and being counted in the exchange (not collapsing to please others). Living in that tension is an ongoing challenge." Mike is talking about being able to hold onto himself without taking other people hostage as he addresses his fear, shame, and other more vulnerable feelings. For men, holding onto ourselves has a lot to do with letting go of our grip on others.

Mike's example is not the only way that codependent behaviors can show up in men's lives. Nate said, "I want to control things. It is hard for me to watch others make decisions I view as unhealthy. My self-esteem can be tied to the relationships in my life. I have a tendency to be insecure and sensitive at times." Like a lot of us men, Nate describes feeling good about himself when people essentially behave the way he wants them to, and feeling bad about himself when those he cares for behave in ways that he deems unhealthy. A part of him feels responsible for the decisions other people make. That is where overly concerned, controlling, and overly critical behavior comes from. I have seen this over and over again with fathers whose child is struggling with addiction. It takes a lot of emotional muscle to detach from others, especially those we love the most, and the decisions they make in their lives.

What will it take for you to hold onto yourself and still feel like a man? Isn't that really the question? How are you going to be true to who you are in your relationships and not let the Rules rule you? There is a balance where you can hold onto yourself *and* who you are as a man. The more you hold onto yourself, the more you can be the man you truly are rather than the one you think others want or need you to be.

Superman

Can't you just see Superman showing up at an Al-Anon meeting:

> "Hi, my name is uh . . . Clark. . . . Well, actually it is . . . Supe . . . Su-per-mah . . . Superman.

> "At first, it was great. All of these people depending on me to save them. I mean, I got to save people's lives. I got to keep bad things from happening. People loved me. You would hear my name everywhere.

> "But . . . but . . . then they expected me to be there. Always. It got to the point where I couldn't have any life for myself.

> "I had a love of my life, Lois, but that fell apart. All of my other guy superheroes told me that she was being clingy and needy and I needed to focus on my work. It is *so* important (he says with a twinge of sarcasm, gesturing with his hands).

"Thanks, everyone, for being here."

The Group: "Keep coming back, Superman!"

And, of course, being Superman, he never went back to that meeting. He came up with all kinds of reasons—not enough time; all those people did was whine about their problems; it actually wasn't that bad, he had just had a moment of weakness—but the truth is, it was just too vulnerable for him. So he put the cape back on, as tight as ever, and was off to "save the day."

Mark talked about his growing awareness about how his need to look good and be viewed as the man who can "save the day" can affect him: "I have seen how my caretaking can be self-destructive when I do not put my own needs as a priority." Mark is an amazing man who is there for everyone. But it comes at a cost, to him and to his relationships. The problem is that men frequently don't see self-care as a priority. In their minds, real men always put the needs of others first. Self-care is code for being weak and whiny.

Bobby talked about how much he has strangled himself with the Superman cape he expected himself to wear constantly: "Trying to 'save' everyone. I have a twenty-year personal history of trying to rescue my AA sponsees, my spouse, my kids, my patients, my coworkers, and all my friends." Sounds exhausting, doesn't it? In what ways is that like your life? I struggled like hell with this when I first got into recovery. I heard people say that I wasn't responsible for another person's recovery, but I didn't quite get it. At the heart of it was my fear that if I didn't help them they would relapse, and if they relapsed they would die, just like my father did. I was a horrible sponsor—always telling the men what to do, judging them, getting angry at them and even yelling, and thinking I knew best. I hid behind my knowledge of the Big Book and the Twelve Steps and Twelve Traditions. I was a controlling SOB with people I cared about, because the bottom line was, I was scared. As a result, they never experienced how much I cared for them. That's how codependency shows up for a lot of men.

The scary thing about the Superman role is that it is not just men who expect this of ourselves; often it is also women. Brené Brown points out in *Men, Women, and Worthiness* how invested so many women are in having men keep the cape on. They have internalized the Man Rules. Is there a safe place for you to talk about how these pressures can feel like kryptonite? Maybe it is not your spouse. Maybe it is your parents or other family members, or your sponsor, or someone else. I highly encourage you to find a resource safe enough for you to speak with about the internal and external pressure you feel to be Superman. Even if you don't have to take the cape off, at least loosen it enough so you can breathe more easily. You can still "save the day"; just put a little more energy into saving yourself, too.

Please Don't Leave Me

The pop artist Pink sings a very powerful song about the challenges she was having in her marriage and all of the pain she was causing her husband and her pushing him away. The song, sung in her raspy and desperate-yet-tough voice, is called "Please Don't Leave Me." I was sitting on an airplane working on this book when this song played through my headphones, and I heard it. I mean I really heard it—and I started crying. On the plane. Not only did this describe how I have treated so many people in my life, but I continue to realize how I have hurt the people I care about most, all because I haven't wanted them to leave me. When I first got into recovery, I would have this feeling before I was even in a relationship or had even spoken to the woman! This had everything to do with me not being able to be okay with me—a problem a lot more men have than are able to see or willing to admit.

The truth is, a lot of us men don't like to admit how much we want and need other people in our lives. Admitting we want others in our lives requires vulnerability. Rod spoke honestly about how this shows up in his life: "I can sacrifice myself for the sake of not being/feeling abandoned." Sacrificing one's own needs for the needs of another or so we can avoid being or feeling alone is codependent. The great irony is that our deep fear of being abandoned leads us to act in ways that push others away—they distance themselves, emotionally at first, and then, often, physically.

I cannot count the number of men I have known and worked with over the years who put vast emotional stock in being accepted by a potential love interest, female or male. The funny thing is, men like to pretend that only women can be that needy or emotionally attached to someone else. When men finally start to acknowledge their own neediness, they typically feel shame because they judge it to be so unmanly. But when they feel safe enough to talk about it, they do. What drives this fragile emotional state for men is the lack of an ability to hold onto themselves. They lose themselves, their self-worth, their self-confidence, and their self-esteem in the absence of signals in the context of a romantic relationship or a potential relationship—a text, phone call, smile, or some other indication that to them affirms their value. These are not weak men. Many of them are "manly" men by most definitions. Call it whatever you want; it is classic codependent behavior. We may come by it honestly, but have been socialized to not acknowledge it. There also comes a time when, as we grow healthier emotionally, we are able to see specific forms of codependent behavior and thinking:

- You find yourself having a pattern of relationships where a person is not available to you emotionally.
- You notice how anxious you get when your loved one is away from you.
- You realize that you have a tendency to let your partner's opinion have excessive influence over things you like and like to do.
- You spend a lot of time trying to get people to like you and validate you as important.

Codependence or Compassion?

Ray seemed to verbalize well that the real challenge is "understanding the difference between codependency and compassion." We do not ever want to stop caring about others. We do not want to ever stop being of service to others and helping them, even when they are capable and competent. But there is a line. Maybe it is also the degree to which we depend on others to take care of us and meet our needs, when we do not hold onto ourselves enough. We cross the line between codependency and compassion when sacrificing our own health and feelings of peace for others becomes a pattern. That line is not static, however. It is different for different men, in different relationships, and even at different points of the same relationship.

An idea I talked about briefly in *A Man's Way through the Twelve Steps* is the continuum of connection: Independence →Interdependence →Codependence. The place on the continuum to strive for is interdependence, a healthy ability to depend on one another, sacrifice for one another, and take care of and hold onto ourselves. Interdependence is about balance. The extremes of both independence and codependence are much less conducive to healthy relationship building. Most people will spend time in all three of the categories on this continuum. Typically, we go back and forth between them. There are occasions when we are more independent, others when we are interdependent, and others when we are more codependent.

I coined the term "relaxed masculinity" to describe how our concepts of masculinity change and soften, allowing us to follow the Man Rules less rigidly. Many of us begin to experience a more relaxed masculinity when we get into recovery, therapy, or some form of personal growth. The ability to wear masculinity as a loose garment also allows us to better practice interdependence—one of the core elements of healthy relationships.

Into Action

▶ Identify two of your closest relationships. Think about times when you had conflict and/or were angry with the other person. Now ask yourself the following questions:
  • What else was going on in that relationship?
  • What feelings were underneath the anger and the conflict (think back to the anger funnel)?
  • What was the person doing?
  • What were you not communicating to them, and why?

▶ Go to an Al-Anon meeting (you can refer to www.alanon. org), preferably a men's meeting if they are available. Talk to two people afterward and ask them what it means to them to consider themselves or their behavior as codependent.

▶ In your journal, reflect on the ideas of being independent, dependent, and interdependent. Write about what each one means to you.

CHAPTER THIRTEEN
Healing Trauma

"I am not afraid to go there or to walk with others who are going through it." –Rod

"Shame still happens but is tolerable, ever a good teacher." –Larry

The first thing that a man has to do in order to heal from trauma he has experienced is to acknowledge that the trauma exists. Nick talked about this when he echoed what I have heard so many men say over the years, many of them long into their personal recovery: "Certainly my sexual abuse was not understood as abuse by me for twenty-plus years." When a man comes to see some part of his life as traumatic, it is a major step, and something that should never be taken lightly.

As I have stated earlier, the best way for a man to continue to suffer as a result of his trauma is to tell himself that he does not have trauma. He may convince himself that trauma is an issue for women and children. Real men don't experience trauma because they are tough. They can handle pain. We are silenced by the chorus of voices telling us to, as Guy said, "suck it up, buttercup." Nate said, "Men tend to deny and look the other way. Admitting they have been traumatized is a blow to the ego and makes men feel powerless." When traumatic experiences and their effects on the internal and interactional lives of men go unrecognized, the wounds are left to fester. When traumatic experiences and their effects are dismissed as unmanly, we experience additional trauma. Emilio said, "I believe our culture of what it means to be a man does not appropriately recognize trauma and its effects." As a result, we hurt ourselves and we hurt other people when we act out on our trauma-driven pain. Jose said, "I think when men are socialized with unhealthy ideas of being a man, they can cause and receive a lot of trauma."

The Rules tell us that the source of our irritation is everyone else, but this only works for so long. Once we begin to travel toward authentic connection with another human being, we step more into our vulnerability and all of the "unfinished business" from our past, mostly our childhood. When the common denominator in the variety of troubles we encounter is us, we have to ask ourselves, *Can it really be everyone else?*

As I described in Chapter Three, the more we move into the depths of intimacy and love, the more our trauma gets triggered, often with us having no awareness of it. A friend of mine told me, "I have heard about that 'family of origin' stuff ever since I got sober, and I always thought it was bullshit. Now, I can see it really has an effect on me. A big one." If we pay attention and are open, there is something very spiritual about it all. This friend and his wife had recently had their second child when someone suggested that he needed to look at some of those issues if he wanted to be a good spouse and father. Chris said, "I have talked a lot about it [trauma] with other men, and I have done a lot of work around the issues I've been through. Once I knew my father was a sick person, I knew that's what it was. I didn't personalize it so much. I have healing to do, but I have to take responsibility for my behavior now as an adult."

The truth is that there is a tremendous amount of trauma in recovery communities. For many people, addiction to substances and behaviors is a way of attempting to escape their pain. There are legions of men living with undiagnosed and untreated trauma in the rooms of recovery. In chaotic families with addiction, abuse, violence, and other dysfunction there is an unspoken conspiracy of silence, denial, mistrust, blame, and emotional deadening. How often do we treat men in the rooms of recovery the same way? How many of us were treated that way? How many of us have internalized all of that pain and darkness? How many of us are simply trying to stay afloat, with all of the baggage that we have been carrying around since we were children weighing us down? There are meetings that are beautiful and full of men striving to heal and become the best men they can be. Yet many of these twelve-step programs are full of wonderful, well-intentioned men (and women) who have no understanding of trauma.

I can't overemphasize that it took me a long time into my recovery to internalize that when it comes to abuse you suffered as a child, in doing the Fourth and Fifth Steps there is no "your part." Sure, you may have made mistakes as a child, but that is what being a child is, and we rely on adults to love us through those mistakes. They do not become the reason later in our lives to excuse or explain why someone abused us. There is nothing, absolutely nothing, that you did to cause what happened to you. There is nothing that excuses abuse, period. If you are not getting that message from the program you're in, your sponsor, or your meeting, then they are doing you, and themselves, a great disservice. If someone wants to get you to look at your behavior as a child, that is fine, but that is separate from the abuse you experienced. Was I a hyper child? Yes. Was I a foul-mouthed kid by the age of seven? Yes. Was I disrespectful to most, if not all, authority? Yes. Does any of that excuse how I was often treated? Unequivocally, no!

Abetted by caricatures such as the Stuart Smalley character on *Saturday Night Live* in the 1990s—an emasculated, effeminate man-boy who belonged to "many twelve-step programs"—the perception of men dealing with our pain and looking at the traumatic pieces of our childhood and adolescence has been lampooned, diminished, and mocked. Although I thought that character was quite funny, for long into my recovery every time I was encouraged to do anything reminiscent of "inner child" work, I could not get Stuart Smalley out of my head. It is really hard to do this intense, painful work that requires making oneself so vulnerable and feel as though our masculinity remains intact. Sean said, "Vulnerability has to be okay. If not, nothing will change." As freeing as it feels to let go of the suffering from our early experiences, we need to find ways to put that work into a context of a healthy masculinity. We are far from truly believing as a society that "real men cry." Hell, there is still a part of me, that part still enslaved by the Rules, that cringes at such a statement. As Mark described it, "We have to let go of the idea of invincibility to see all our potential for growth."

Untreated trauma remains in our body, our mind, and our spirit. What I would have given to have had someone who really understood men's trauma to help me when I first entered recovery. I grieve the impact that had on all of my relationships and the loss of time, a lot of which I spent harboring this secret conversation inside me thinking I was crazy. That being said, I do believe that everything happened just as it was supposed to for me. But that doesn't mean it has to be the same for other men, including you. In recovery we talk about having gotten free that we might free others. I add to that: that we might free them *even sooner.*

As I noted earlier, I was ten years in recovery before someone mentioned the idea of trauma to me, and it happened then only because my therapist had just attended a training focused on trauma. It took another four years of intensive work, during which I experienced a whole new bottom, for me to get through the shame of my various traumas. That bottom was facing the difficulties in my marriage because of my continuing struggles with anger. I do not like to admit it. I do not want to admit it. But talking about it and owning it is necessary to heal from it. Owning my story and bringing it out into the light in an environment of emotional safety and acceptance is what kills the shame.

It is only in the past two years that I have felt myself becoming fully freed from the grip of trauma and its impacts on my life and my behavior. It was when I saw the beginning glimmers of me treating my daughter the way I had been treated growing up that I finally surrendered. We cannot will trauma away. We will never heal on the basis of self-knowledge alone. We cannot think, talk, pray, or work the steps to find our way out of trauma. All of that helps and is necessary, but it is not sufficient. My trauma recovery has continued, sometimes quickly and sometimes slowly, and seems to have saved my marriage and ensured that I will not follow in my father's footsteps when it comes to parenting.

Some men have many layers of trauma. Others have some very acute trauma that may be more easily resolved. I do believe that we must talk to every man in treatment about trauma and plant the seed as soon as possible. In talking with men about trauma, we have to talk to them about being men, and about being men with trauma, and what that means to them. Just as shame is a gendered construct, so is trauma. How does a man feel about being a man when admitting he was abused? What is it like for a man to cry in front of other men? What stories does a man make up about his being a man as a result of beginning to look at his abuse? What Rules are getting in the way of his being able to do this work? These are some of the questions we need to explore along the journey of healing from trauma.

The Core Principles of Healing Trauma

In the past two decades, as treatment providers have begun to understand what it means to be trauma-informed and to incorporate this understanding into their services, some guiding principles have been developed. These come from the seminal work of Maxine Harris and Roger Fallot. These principles can also apply to twelve-step recovery communities and our relationships within those communities. The five main principles, though there are many more, are Safety, Trustworthiness, Collaboration, Choice, and Empowerment. I would also add Responsibility and Compassion as two principles that are very important for men. I will talk briefly about each one, as they are essential in identifying the support necessary to help you heal from trauma.

If you think about the environments in which one experiences trauma, they are the opposite of all of those principles—there is no safety and no trust, there is usually a very rigid system, people feel powerless and hopeless, and everyone feels alone, not as though they are truly part of a family. The question is, how can a therapist's office or the rooms of recovery feel or even be similar at times?

Safety

Safety is, and will always be, the number-one principle. I point out all the time how unlikely it is that men will admit that we do not feel safe.

Paradoxically, we have to feel incredibly safe to admit how unsafe we feel. Otherwise, our lack of feeling safe will lead us to protect ourselves, sometimes by acting out in ways that work against creating safety for us and others in our lives. How safe do you feel in your meetings or with your therapist? How safe do you feel talking about what is really going on without having some "oldtimer" say to you directly or passive-aggressively that you just need to work the steps harder, surrender more, or have more gratitude?

Trustworthiness

Trustworthiness is critical to any relationship. When you build a relationship with another man in recovery, the pact is that you have their confidence; you can trust them not to betray you. Trust is based on confidence that we will do no harm to one another and that we will do what we say we are going to do. If we say we are going to call, we call. If we say we are going to pick someone up, then we pick them up. If we agree to sponsor someone, then we make ourselves available or we help him find someone else. Part of how we learn to trust each other is by listening compassionately and without judgment to what men have to share in meetings. Through such experiences we learn that we will not be laughed at, ridiculed, or shamed for sharing our pain openly.

Collaboration

Collaboration might be applied to your relationship with your sponsor: Is it one of those relationships where you are always one peg down from him? Do you feel like you are a team, or it is more like a sergeant and a private? There may always be a time when our sponsor needs to confront us and take a more directive role, but for the most part a collaborative approach helps to create a sense of respect. A lot of men are afraid that if they do this with the men they sponsor, they are going to take advantage of them. A lot of sponsors get some sort of ego trip from being able to talk down to a sponsee and treat them as though they have nothing to offer and no inherent wisdom of their own.

Choice

Choice can be seen as giving a man some choice in the matter of the path and timeline of his recovery, whether it be through counseling, twelve-step recovery, other mutual support groups, engagement in a faith community, or some combination of the four. We so often talk about twelve-step programs as a "design for living." This is very true according to the experience of the men I interviewed. But what does that mean? Is the design the same for everyone? Perhaps in a broad way, but not always in the details. The key is for men to have the ultimate choice— the choice to take 100 percent responsibility for their lives and to begin to truly cultivate their own emotional self.

Empowerment

Empowerment is a counterweight for male survivors of trauma who go through a lot of their lives feeling powerless, regardless of how they may present. We can perpetuate this feeling in all sorts of ways, from initial intervention to long into recovery. Males who have spent so much of their lives attempting to navigate severe anxiety, dissociation, rage, isolation, and feelings of powerlessness need to feel some healthy connection to power. I have talked about this in several chapters. Empowerment is not some flowery word; it is an important part of a man grabbing onto his recovery and feeling as though he matters and belongs.

Accountability vs. Responsibility

How is *accountability* different from responsibility? Although they are related, responsibility is broader. Am I the one who made that mistake? Am I the one who failed to meet the deadline I had agreed to? We live in a world of blame, where everyone is quick to point fingers and blame someone else when something goes wrong or when problems occur. Accountability means my ego and my need to maintain a particular reputation are not greater than my willingness to say, "Yes, I did that." Being responsible is how I build a truly respectful and meaningful reputation. It is partially through *responsibility* that we achieve integrity. When I acknowledge that I was responsible, and I failed to honor that responsibility, it enhances my integrity. Emilio said, "If my integrity is high, accountability isn't much of an issue."

Compassion

A model I use based Cindy Wigglesworth's work is that there are probably four different experiences in relationships with respect to relating to another's distress or suffering: apathy, sympathy, empathy, and compassion. Apathy is lacking feelings for something, not really caring. Sympathy is feeling sorry for someone. We feel *for* them, often without really taking the time to understand what is happening to or with them. In contrast, empathy is when we feel *with* someone as a result of having had similar experiences through which we can more deeply understand their feelings. Finally, compassion is connected to some kind of action. In the Buddhist conception, when we have compassion for someone as we truly "see" them, we are moved to do something to help ease their suffering.

A challenge within the twelve-step community is that some of us are invested in telling others what they need to do because we think we know. Without seeing that person and what is happening in their life at that moment, we simply parrot back certain seemingly fitting well-worn sayings or slogans like "You need to surrender," or "Work the steps," or "This too shall pass," or whatever. But if we have not heard or seen the person in that moment in their suffering, there can be no true compassion. Nick said that compassion "helps me be connected to others in their experience." *Their* experience, not mine. Men are especially predisposed toward this because we "fix" things, and in our need to "fix" the situation we often let our arrogance, our need to be right, and our belief that we know what's best get in the way of being present with those still suffering.

You must cultivate your capacity for compassion if you are going to grow in your relationships. It is important to have compassion for yourself, as well as the one with whom you are in relationship. Nobody practices all of these principles in all of their affairs, nor does anyone practice any of them perfectly—but we strive to. I constantly fail in implementing these principles, but I see—and address—that failure much more often than I used to. I also am rarely fettered by shame anymore to prevent me from seeing my behavior outside my own self-centered and self-obsessed selfishness. All of that progress is a direct result of the compassion others have shown me and taught me how to give to myself. Out of that compassion has come the ability for me to do the next indicated thing.

The collective wisdom of the men I interviewed made it clear that compassion is something that one gains for people when they share themselves openly and vulnerably. Mike said, "Compassion happens when we share at the deepest levels." When a person shares openly and vulnerably their truest self, how can you not feel a deep connection to them that says, "I am with you"? I *suffer with* you; let us walk together through it.

Sobriety Is Necessary . . . but Not Sufficient

At some point everyone who is sober will ask him- or herself, "Is this all there is?" The answer may surprise you. If you discover trauma and the impact it has had on your life, the answer will become quite clear. That answer is not to work the steps harder. The answer is not to go to more meetings. Or do more service work. Or get more sponsees. Or stop being so self-centered. Nor is it simply to pray. Or even meditate. The answers may be all of the above, but not the above *only*.

The steps are a powerful force to aid in the healing of trauma, but are likely to be limited in what they can do to effect the needed change in our brains, particularly in repairing the disconnect between the prefrontal cortex and the limbic system and the effects of the trauma stuck in our bodies.

I have watched many men fall. Many good men. Some, like my father, never really ever had a chance, while others are tortured long into their recovery by the ghosts of trauma that are constantly whispering in their ear and having them question their sanity. We have to end the collusion among so many men that says, "I won't confront you on the unhealthy behavior of your recovery (sex addiction, porn addiction, gambling, rage, abusiveness)," often as a result of untreated trauma. We have to acknowledge that emotional recovery and trauma work are inextricably connected. If this revolution is going to come to fruition, then we have to acknowledge that sobriety is necessary but not sufficient.

The Crucible

There is a joke in recovery: If you want to see the quality of your recovery, just get into a relationship. Everything happens in the context of relationships. All of our relationships, especially our most personal ones, are constantly in motion. Our most intimate relationships are the crucible of self-discovery. You will always have connection and disconnection; the question is, what do you cocreate to be able to heal through the disconnection and strengthen the connection?

Relationships are also the crucible for unearthing trauma. Trauma that has been leaking out for years may now come gushing out, seemingly out of the blue. Men are dying—literally—to let their pain and suffering out. We do it in relationships, sometimes when it is safe to do so and sometimes when it is not. We take risks, and sometimes they work and sometimes they do not. As we move further into the intimacy, we move further into vulnerability and automatically increase the possibility of disconnection—so we can protect ourselves.

If you believe, as many of the great spiritual teachers do, that we invite people into our lives to help us heal and grow, then our partners are our teachers. Nancy and I had a couples counselor who explained to us that you can think of people as vessels that are full to varying degrees based upon their own development and differentiation. He went on to say that we tend to find partners whose "vessels" are at about the same level as ours, no matter how it may appear on the surface. The mistake, however, would be to then conclude that our partner is the one who can fill us up. The goal is for us to join together in a shared journey of finding ways to get our vessels filled.

Good Grief

In trauma work, grief is a major force in the healing process, especially for men. If you watch a man in his first couple of days in addiction treatment, you will see the effects of grief. It may start with the grief that men begin to get in touch with as they let go of their addictive substances or behaviors. Some of it is the grief related to all that his addiction has taken from him and from his loved ones and his relationships with them. But that is just the tip of iceberg. Grief applies to so many things. The following is a short list of the kinds of losses about which men may experience grief:

- Deaths of loved ones
- Ending of significant relationships
- Abuse and violence that has been perpetrated on us
- Any kind of social marginalization we may have experienced growing up
- Our loss of childhood
- Moving; loss of home, place, friends
- The way we were raised as men
- Violence that we have perpetrated on others
- The loss of our addictive substances
- Any number of actions we took while active in our addiction that violated our values or hurt people
- Miscarriages, aborted pregnancies (particularly those in which we were given no say)
- For combat veterans of war, actions taken as part of that process
- Loss of jobs or livelihood
- Loss of hopes, dreams for the future
- Aging

I remember working in treatment and seeing some men who seemed to be bursting at the seams with grief. In some cases it only took one group or individual session for these men to begin to express their grief and deep sense of loss. They were exceptions to the Rule: Big boys don't cry. Most men leave treatment not having touched their grief because treatment programs rarely prioritize it. Although some men aren't yet ready to acknowledge and express their grief, no one should leave treatment without having multiple opportunities to begin looking at his grief.

Grief is another portal to vulnerability. Since vulnerability is often equated with weakness, expressing one's natural grief is, for many, a violation of the Man Rules. As such, grief is something men are not allowed to feel. During our childhood most of us were told directly and indirectly to "stop crying or I'll give you something to cry about." Even more enlightened fathers often struggle with their sons' emotionality, trying to figure out how to honor it without making them "too weak." They may not do some of the traditional "greatest hits" of fathers who verbally beat their sons into emotional submission, but they still struggle with this more with their sons than they do with their daughters. The effects of these early experience are lifelong. Even some of the healthiest men I know, especially those not in twelve-step recovery, still struggle with allowing themselves to show their grief and sadness.

David talked about the amount of grief that so many men carry around inside them, long into their recovery: "Lots of grief and loss to work through. Cycles of death and dying. The abuse, cancer, being a man who has sex with men and the society hating that, being black in America, not being smart, not getting through school, and my mother leaving. I continue to work through all of it." The key is that you have to give yourself permission to (1) acknowledge those experiences as painful and traumatic, and (2) grieve them. Those who belong to marginalized groups, such as gay men, men of color, and gay men of color, have unique experiences of grief as a result. Think about it: David is a gay black man, which means he has experienced discrimination and disconnection specific to living in a predominantly heterosexist and homophobic society where racism is still present. Finally, he is also marginalized in both of those groups because he is still the "other," a black man in a gay man's community and a gay man in a black man's (read: hypermasculine) community. Shit, that is a lot to walk through. Many men carry multiple layers of grief with them, even those men you'd never expect knew anything about suffering.

As a Native American, Okwas talked about the intergenerational grief connected with the intergenerational trauma his people experienced and the impact that has had on him personally: "Too many have died in my life because of the trauma effects of residential schools. In my grandfather and grandmother's generation there are over five hundred from the schools, and one hundred have passed away. Each one was close to me. I used to have five brothers and two sisters; I now have one brother and one sister left. I lost a son and five other family members in a house fire in 1988. Grief and loss are like an onion; you peel one layer off and there's still another layer there. All 1 know is that if I depend on the Great Spirit to walk me through it, then it will be okay." This is a powerful example of a culturally specific trauma that other cultures may know little about. Ed shared, "We lost over forty-five men in my gay AA community during the peak of AIDS. I lost my best friend, my father, a relationship only made possible through our mutual recoveries. My younger brother was murdered, the worst loss and most profound grief to date." Part of the healing process is to create a space for men to talk about their pain, whatever that pain is. We don't have to understand it or fix it; we just have to listen and be witnesses.

If you are a man in recovery, you have grief related to the losses you've experienced. If you think you have worked through all of your grief, look again as fearlessly and thoroughly as you are able—there may be more there than you realized. Furthermore, the longer you stay in recovery and remain connected to the twelve-step community, the more loss you will experience from people dying from overdoses, suicide, and other effects of addiction. You are not likely to go through your recovery without losing at least one person close to you to relapse or some other fatal side effect of their addiction. In twenty years I have grieved the deaths of two sponsees; four close friends; several colleagues who were also friends, including one of the men interviewed for this book; and numerous acquaintances. Sadly, it comes with the territory.

Bob talked about dealing with grief as a practice that involves developing a set of skills: "My experience with these losses and the loss of friends along the way has made me believe that learning to deal with loss in the most skillful way is my major task in life." Nick also alluded to the fact that learning how to grieve is a practice: "Early on, accessing the sadness was quite difficult. I had to practice crying. I do okay with both now." Note that he said "okay," not "awesome," nor did he suggest that he has mastered the skill.

Roland spoke for a lot of men when he said, "I wish I could cry more, but the tears and emotions dissipate and I can't access them anymore." It has taken almost two decades for me to get my tears back. So many men cannot access their tears, their grief, or simply their sadness because there is such an ingrained sense that they reflect weakness and are therefore unacceptable. The greatest challenge about grief, especially for men, is giving ourselves permission not just to talk about it (though that is the all-important first step), but also to feel it. Men in recovery who "know the program" are really good at knowing exactly what to say. Gary described the struggle that men have in feeling grief and sadness. His comments are indicative of the influence of the anger funnel: "Dealing with my emotions and feelings can be challenging as a man because it tends to bring up character defects such as anger. When a man's recovery moves from his head to his heart, he can't but help get in touch with his grief—anger is no longer a viable wall for us to hide our pain behind."

Of course, it is not just other men who can sometimes have a difficult time with a man's grief. Chris said the hardest thing about being a man and grieving was "feeling self-conscious about feeling it all in the presence of a woman." How many men can identify with that statement? Whether it is a man's own fear of being judged negatively or a woman's internalization of the Rules that leads to an actual negative judgment, it can take a lot for men to feel safe enough to share their grief with their female partners. In many men's minds, it is the ultimate confession of "not being a man."

Jose said, "Outward grief is still looked down upon by society if you're a man. I really think we still have strides to make in this area as a society." Sean talked about the fear of and actual experience of "judgment from other men" when he allows himself to touch the grief he carries with him. At some point a man has to decide what is more important—the Rules or sharing himself authentically with his loved ones. Larry talked about the importance of "learning to overcome the perception that a man cannot grieve openly."

Bob also talked about the way men are expected to deal with grief in our society: "Men buck up, men get over it, men stay strong, and men stay quiet about it." In other words, men do not deal with their grief. Remember, grief and loss are not just about men crying or learning to cry. It is about us giving ourselves permission to acknowledge that loss is an essential part of life, and the more you open your heart, the more you open your life to the possibility of loss.

David described the struggle he has as a man in dealing with grief as "being gentle with that part of me that isn't tough." The self-compassion that David speaks of is essential. We need to learn how to be loving and accepting toward ourselves in our grief.

We give grief and the need to grieve short shrift in our society. We allow people about a month to get over a loss, and maybe two to three months if it is a serious loss. But anyone who has actually waded through the stormy waters of grief knows that it is something that changes you forever. I am not talking about merely talking about grieving, I am talking about really wading through it—up to your neck. I know for myself this can take years. My father died almost twenty years ago and I am still grieving him. It comes up every time Grace talks about her grandparents and asks, "I have two grandmas. Why don't I have two grandpas?" There are many experiences that remind me of everything we never had as well as some of the precious moments where I got to experience the man my father was, outside of the sickness of his alcoholism. I would be surprised if there is not some sadness and loss until the day I die.

Earl said it beautifully: "I've become a better and more intentional griever. I don't avoid the painful parts of my life. I'm okay being with pain and an emotional mess when that is appropriate." Earl embraces the experiences of loss in his life because he knows that it is a part of who he is and a part of life. Fighting it is a losing battle. Surrendering to it is transformative.

Nate said it best: "I have learned that I can survive loss and that it is okay to feel sad. At the same time, I can be strong for others." We can allow ourselves to experience the grief we need to while also being supportive to others. Luke said, "I've learned in recovery and my emotional work that grief will not drown me or kill me. There is a gift available for me if I choose to dive in and discover it." There is no question that a lot of men fear that their grief will drown them because they have some sense of how much pain they have been stuffing down deep inside them for most of their life. That is daunting.

Mark said what helped him deal with grief most was "knowing I will be okay no matter what." It will not consume us. We can go through the process of fully acknowledging and grieving our losses, and we will be okay. It may bring you to your knees. You may cry so hard you feel like you are never going to stop, but you will. And afterward, the feeling of letting all of that pain out is amazing. As my friend Wanda, a retired stripper from Kansas City, used to say, "It's just like taking a shower on the inside." If you would like to read more on this topic, I refer you to the chapter "Men and Grief" in *A Man's Way through the Twelve Steps.*

Trauma and Forgiveness

There is no question that forgiveness is an advanced concept when it comes to trauma. It can also be quite controversial, mostly because of what forgiveness is and is asking from an individual. It is a spiritual principle that is less cognitive than it is emotional, and even existential. It often comes down to forgiving God, ourselves, and/or the perpetrator of behavior that traumatized us (if applicable). Forgiveness has special importance in the twelve-step community in that seeking and offering forgiveness is rooted in Steps Eight and Nine. A saying I first heard in recovery has stuck with me: "Forgiveness is not forgetting; it is letting go of the hurt." I will never tell a man that he has to forgive anyone. It is sad to see some men hang onto the hatred and anger they have toward their fathers or others who have harmed them because they cannot see how much that hatred and anger is harming them.

It does seem that by working the steps people will often come to some place of forgiveness. The more times you go through the steps, the stronger your interest in cultivating forgiveness is likely to become, because you begin to see those who have harmed you more clearly. Grief work also seems to be something that leads us toward a path of forgiveness. Grief helps us to cultivate compassion. We see how much pain we have been carrying and we become more and more committed to being free of it.

And the freedom forgiveness can provide is profound. I was at an event in Minneapolis where the keynote speaker was a woman whose son had been killed by a local gang member. She visited the man, in prison, who killed her son and began to get to know him. She not only got to know him, but she came to forgive him and adopt him as her son. They now speak together all over the country about the epidemic of violence in the inner city and the power of forgiveness.

Forgiveness is a process more than an event. Rod said, "Learning to forgive has been a lifelong journey." Something shifted for me when it came to my father and the abuse I experienced at his hands. It may have been the numerous letters I wrote to him, each one helping me to see him and the pain I had around our relationship more clearly. It may have been the prayers and talking to and yelling at my father since his death. It may have been the hours of grief work I have done around our relationship. But today I am able to see my father as a very wounded man who never really lived. Everything he did to me, he was not doing to me, per se. He was acting out against everything that he hated about himself and all that had been destroyed inside him as a child. That does not excuse his behavior at all, but it does help me to see that he was not the man or the father he wanted to be. As a result, I can honestly say that I love my father and feel great sadness for the relationship we were never able to have. I can also say that I have mostly forgiven him for every trespass. I am not sure how it has happened other than that I have gradually let go of the hurt, and as a result of that my heart has opened.

You get to decide how you want to approach any of the abuse that happened to you. There may truly be some things that cannot be forgiven. Some men I know, who have survived truly horrific and unspeakable abuse, have helped me to see that forgiveness may not always be what is called for. There is a place for acceptance of what happened, but not forgiveness, they have told me. Not having to walk in their shoes, who am I to judge that? Forgiveness is a sacred journey that only you can truly walk. My only suggestion is to approach it with as open a heart as you are able.

The Rules definitely get in the way of our ability to clearly see the impact that trauma has had on our lives. Ricardo said, "Men are typically disconnected from their feelings in general, and with the emotional numbness of trauma and the hyperarousal states, men can act out on their trauma without learning how to deal with their internal process." At the time of this writing I am engaged in a process of EMDR therapy to deal with some of the deeper layers of my life story and how these have haunted me and my self-perception. Most of it revolves around the impact the growth problem I experienced in high school had on my self-concept and how it affected my sense of self as a man, my perception of my body, and my challenges to connect with Nancy without having a traumatic reaction every time I am vulnerable with her. It is yet another layer of the false sense of reality I constructed a long time ago in order to try to make sense of my world. But it is time to let it go once and for all.

Remember, the key factor in understanding trauma is that it has everything to do with the individual's response to the event. How a child responds to an event can lead to the development of trauma. That trauma is not eliminated because the adult version of that person decides that, for any number of reasons, it was "not a big deal." The wound is still there, and either we honor the wound and own it, or it owns us. Bob said about his own trauma, "There seem to be more layers and layers, but it's not as charged as it once was." We may have layers of trauma, but we can get through them. One layer at a time. You can get through them. Not by yourself, but with the help of supportive and knowledgeable others and your Higher Power, you can do it. I was sitting with a man who has worked with men in prison and jail for decades, and he said, "My wounding happened amongst people; my healing must happen amongst people."

Happy, Joyous, and (Truly) Free

When it comes to moving toward health and wholeness, the concept of layers makes great sense. On that note, have you ever noticed how many layers there are to ideas in twelve-step programs of recovery? Take, for instance, the pithy little saying that headlines this section. I am constantly amazed at how my experience of happiness, joy, and freedom changes the more I grow. Happiness used to simply mean the absence of depression. Freedom was the ability to walk down the street with my head up or to be able to leave my apartment without some major self-talk drama. Today, all three of these areas have expanded, deepened, and blossomed into concepts and possibilities I could not have foreseen.

Today, happiness means that I have discovered an inner peace and calm that is much more present in my life than it ever was. I can sit alone in my hotel room and not need anything to distract me. I still have bouts with fear, insecurity, and self-doubt. But this doesn't paralyze me. It doesn't define me anymore. I don't tend to struggle against it anymore; instead, I acknowledge and often share it with someone else. I try to talk about feeling shame and hurt rather than simply acting like an asshole. I still make mistakes. I still lose my temper, but I recognize it and clean it up sooner than I ever have.

My point in talking about this is that I have seen far too many men who have been in recovery for years or even decades for whom the idea of being "happy, joyous, and free" has been limited by their inability to acknowledge the depth of their suffering. Bob said, "Healing is a journey for me. Today I have more moments of relaxation in my own body, more joy and gratitude, more emotional expressiveness within myself and with others, and more acceptance of my sexual self. Less need to be perfect." I know Bob well enough to know he speaks the truth of who he is, not just who he wishes he was. I know he has done the work. Five years from now I will look back at these words and my experience of "happy, joyous, and free" will be completely different, as more layers will have been shed, and that excites me.

The Missing Peace

Growing up, when I went to church we would often sing a song: *Let there be peace on Earth and let it begin with me.* I always liked the song, but I did not understand how important peace is to our internal world until I began to do trauma work and began to heal. I walked around with so much anger, fear, and cynicism for so long that I didn't know what a real sense of peace was. When I began to truly feel peace inside myself I began to appreciate what it means to my family, our home, our community, and this world.

It has been a long road, and there have been many times when it felt too hard and I wanted to give up, but I didn't, because I have always had people to help me. Sometimes they have pointed me in the right direction, sometimes they have walked with me, and sometimes they have even carried me. But I have always found my way, and I trust that as long as I stay connected to the people who care about me and to my

Higher Power, I will continue to do so. That means you can find peace too, because there is absolutely nothing amazing or special about me—at least not anything more amazing or special than you. I have nothing that you don't also have.

You deserve to have peace. You deserve to be able to look in the mirror and love the man you see. You deserve to feel connected with others at the level your heart desires. You deserve to love all the parts of you that were not loved. Trust that if you step honestly and earnestly into this journey, you will find what you need. The people you need will arrive. The resources you need will be available. It will take time and may not happen as soon as you'd like, but if you stay connected and stay committed to your recovery, it will happen. And when you are standing on the other side of it, when you look back on your journey and see the landscape you have traveled and the obstacles you have overcome, it will all have been worth it. There may be other mountains in front of you, but you will know that you can climb them and you will cherish every step along the way. You will begin to see that the pain of the healing process is as beautiful as the joy of it. You will see that the work you are doing, you are doing for others as much as yourself. And you will pass this on. You will begin to step into the mystery of life and feel deep inside you that All Truly Is Well.

Professionally Driven Trauma Treatment

There are many excellent interventions for treating trauma. Finding the right therapist and modality for you can make all the difference in the world. You are the consumer, so you have the right to interview professionals to make sure they are a good fit. You have the right to ask about their education, level of experience and training, and even what personal work they have done. If professionals are resistant or overly defensive when you ask about these areas, that is a pretty good sign that they are not who you want. An environment of emotional safety is critical to healing trauma, and you need an environment where you are safe and feel safe. That looks different for different people. You know better than anyone if a male or female therapist is going to work better for you.

Listed on the next page are some of the different modalities for treating trauma. I encourage you to do your own research and talk to people you know who have done their own work around trauma and find out what worked and didn't work for them. You can find information and resources on the Internet, including more information about those listed here, as well as how to find professionals trained in this work in your community.

Eye Movement Desensitization and Reprocessing (EMDR)
Brain Spotting
Bio/Neurofeedback
Somatic Experiencing (SE)
Neurolinguistic Programming (NLP)
Emotional Freedom Techniques (EFT)
Thought-Field Therapy (TFT)
Exposure Therapy
Trauma-Focused Cognitive Behavioral Therapy
Hypnotherapy
Art Therapy
Narrative Therapy
Dialectical Behavioral Therapy
Energy Psychology
Trauma Releasing Exercises (TRE)
Gestalt Therapy
Guided Imagery
Mindfulness
Psychodrama

Into Action

I encourage you to research these and other resources, reach out to professionals in your area, and look into getting help if you have any questions about the potential impacts of trauma in your life. You deserve to have peace and fulfilling relationships.

CHAPTER FOURTEEN
Final Thoughts on Men and Relationships

"I have my heart open to relationships. Before, my heart was closed; now, even though I am afraid at times, I open my heart up and let love in." —Okwas

"The breadth and depth of my relationships in sobriety is greater than anything that I could possibly have imagined." —Emilio

My hope is that you have been reading with an open mind and an awareness of how the Man Rules filter so much of our experience in life. There is no doubt in my mind that the Rules have crept up numerous times while you have been reading this book, possibly leading you to negatively judge or dismiss some of the ideas within it, or even me. That's okay. Remember, that's how the Rules work. Hell, the same thing has happened to me while I have been writing this book! That is how powerful the Rules are. Hopefully, you have been able to notice when the Rules were influencing you and you have been able to step back, if only a little bit, to see these ideas clearly.

Let's face it: Relationships are hard. They are hard for men and women. As one woman said to me after one of my trainings, "We all need help with relationships. Women are just as clueless about creating truly intimate, healthy, and loving relationships." I was talking to a woman the other day about her relationship with her fiancé, and it was clear from her comments that she expected him to show up in a relationship based on what the Rules prescribed. She wanted her fiancé to follow the Rules because to her it said something about the kind of man he was, and the kind of man she wanted to be with.

As I've stated, the Rules create unhealthy expectations for both men and women. The truth is that creating and maintaining healthy intimate relationships is a collaborative learning process—no matter with whom we are in relationship, be it our spouse/partner, friends, sponsor, or child(ren). Bobby talked about how his insecurity and shame were influenced by the Rules, leading him to be in constant competition with other men when what he really wanted was connection: "My need to compete instead of collaborate inevitably leads me to self-defeating patterns and strategies, and ineffective outcomes."

The Rules are burned into our mental and emotional hard drives, and we cannot wish them away. They live in our psyches, and many men have taken them on as part of who they are. They have not necessarily chosen to incorporate them into their lives; it has happened through socialization, messaging, and training in childhood and adolescence. Awareness is your most important tool on this journey toward healthy relationships. I do not think the Rules ever completely leave us. I want to figure out a way to have them in my life that works for me and with who I am authentically. Are there times I need to be strong? Of course. If I walked around emoting all of the time, nobody would want to be around me. Just like me, you get to determine how you want the Rules to show up in your life. It is a personal decision that only you can make based on what feels best for you—there are no "right" answers.

The longer I am alive, the more I am convinced life is about balance. Our problem is that we have lost balance. We often have men puffing up their chests, still trying to be lord of the manor while on the other end we have some men who have become so passive that they interpret being a partner as an excuse not to speak up or stand up in their relationship, own their part, ask for what they need, or assert themselves and make decisions. Both extremes are out of balance. If you are a slave to the Man

Rules, you will never have balance or happiness in your relationships. My wish for you is to find balance in who you are and in your relationships.

A New Freedom and a New Happiness

When we were active in our addiction, our relationships suffered greatly. As Roland put it, "I was a cheater, and I was unfaithful to them all (partner, friends, parents, children), because my attention was always on my addiction." That statement speaks to the experience of so many of us. Despite our greatest intentions, during our active addiction pretty much everyone consistently came in second—at best—behind alcohol and other drugs.

Every relationship can be healed. We can learn how to be the best men we can be in every relationship we have, from our partner to the person we see regularly at our local grocery store. Gary said, "Prior to recovery I found myself in relationships where I was unable to communicate my feelings. Either my relationships would be based on fear of someone leaving me or I would tend to use another person for personal gain. I was incapable of being honest about how I felt and what I would like from a relationship." When men get into recovery we get the opportunity and the support to grow the skills that make relationships successful. We learn how to show up honestly in our relationships by looking at our motives and gaining new skills, including the ability to share how we really feel. The majority of men care deeply about our relationships and want to learn more and be able to apply that learning to our most important relationships and, in fact, to all of our relationships.

The road of recovery is paved with many forms of learning and growth. Bobby said, "Emotional sobriety has taught me that my greatest regrets are also my greatest gifts in life. We are connected to one another through our woundedness. While we may admire strength and skill, we are drawn to what's vulnerable and broken in one another. In this way, my wounds are my gift to others, especially to my fellow men, who suffer in silence and apart from one another. I am defined by how my pain has served to benefit others with whom I come into contact."

If you want to have a quality recovery, you have to give yourself permission not only to care about your relationships but also to let others know how much you care and let how much they care into your heart.

Gary said, "My relationships in recovery have been the greatest asset I have. Today I am able to express my feelings and emotions with others without the fear of being judged. I am also able to share my experiences with others in a helpful way, without feelings of guilt or shame."

If you're anything like me, as you have been reading this book you have had moments of truth where you see yourself at your best and your worst. That is how we show up in the world as human beings.

Man Rules, Schman Rules

I am sometimes accused of putting too much emphasis on gender and the Man Rules. Plenty of men have told me that the Man Rules don't affect them, and never have. Others tell me that recovery has helped them to "let all of that go." Others say that focusing on a binary concept of gender is too limiting. I cannot say what is true for any of them. I can only speak from my own experience, which is constantly reaffirmed as I talk to other men from all walks of life about their experiences. I can also guarantee you this: If you have never looked at your ideas of being a man and what beliefs you have created around those ideas, they control you much more than you realize.

Addiction provides an instructive example of how this process works. Before we found recovery, we may have had fleeting glimpses of the damage our addiction was doing to our lives and the lives of those we loved. It wasn't until we stopped using and began to take an open and honest look at ourselves and our behavior that we began to see the real truth. That was only the beginning. As our minds clear and our powers of discernment increase, we see more and more clearly the impact of our addiction. As we look through the lens of recovery, we are able to accurately see just how deeply our active addiction was embedded in our lives. It was there, all right—but we were unable to see it. But seeing our addiction doesn't make it go away. Recovery is a long process of changing—our thinking, how we deal with our feelings, and our behavior.

I believe that is how the Man Rules operate in our lives and negatively impact our relationships. Obviously, the Rules affect individual men in different ways and to very different degrees. Because of my experiences with abuse growing up and the growth problem I endured in adolescence and the trauma it created, I may be on the far end of the continuum. Yet the reality remains for all men that from infancy the Rules are so deeply embedded in our sense of who we are as men—through the direct and indirect messages we have received and internalized—that we are generally unable to see how they influence us and our participation in relationships. And in order to have healthier and more intimate relationships, we need to change.

How do you hold back from expressing and being yourself as a result of your concerns about how you will look as a man? You may say that your concerns are more about how you will look in general, with little or none of it having to do with being a man. That is where I challenge you to simply look. There is no harm in making a good-faith effort, and there is nothing to be gained—other than greater freedom, greater peace, and a greater sense of who you are, if there is something there. If there is not, God bless you, for you are the exceedingly rare exception to the Rules.

This book is relatively meaningless if you don't put these ideas, and others you get from the supportive and wise people in your life, into action! I know so many men who know this information, but when the moment comes and they have to cross the wide chasm between the head and the heart and place themselves vulnerably in the hands of their loved one, they are unable to do it. Keep in mind that at the heart of a lot of relationship dysfunction is trauma—often unrecognized and unaddressed.

There is a really good reason why the end of each chapter has exercises I have encouraged you to do. We have a saying in twelve-step recovery that you cannot think your way into a better way of living, but you can live your way into a better way of thinking. There is real truth to that statement. How many of us had wonderful insights into how screwed up our lives were while we continued to make bad decisions, use, and act out? We did not know how to put our understanding into practice. How many of us have had similar experiences when it comes to relationships?

I cannot tell you how many times I would advise clients (when I worked in direct services) and other men in recovery, especially sponsees, on their relationships while unable to put those same ideas into practice in my own relationships, especially with Nancy. I'd wax philosophical about the importance of having your partner feel loved and doing the little things that could engender that feeling, but did I do it? I always had a reason why I didn't. Everything I share here that I have actually started implementing in my life has made amazing differences in the relationship Nancy and I have.

Every day I am with Grace I realize how important it is for me to focus on growing in my relationship with myself, my God, Nancy, and, of course, Grace. She watches everything I do, as well she should. As James Baldwin said, "Children have never been very good at listening to their elders, but they have never failed to imitate them." What this means for me is that Grace is learning and will continue to learn about how to view and relate to men mostly from me. She is going to develop a self-concept based upon Nancy's and my constant interaction with her as she begins to discover more and more about who she is, separate from us.

A Long Way to Go

I often tell people that a lot of my work comes from a feminist perspective, which gets different kinds of reactions. I explain that feminism simply means that I believe (1) men and women are inherently equal, and (2) we live in a society that is far from acknowledging that truth politically, socially, and interpersonally. Men and women are equal *and* different. This view can lead men to realize that, even if they do not see themselves as endorsing feminism, they nonetheless agree with its central tenets. It should not have to be so significant that we create a space in our world to acknowledge and honor that women are equal.

It also has to be acknowledged that around the world there is still a war against girls and women that is horrific and claims victims every day. Women are far from being free in many countries where basic human dignities are denied to them. Education and the ability to choose a husband are unavailable to women in certain countries. Others routinely practice female genital mutilation. Sexual slavery and human trafficking, which also affects boys and men, is epidemic in many parts of the world, and the buying and selling of children as if they are chattel is feeding the pornography business.

David said the biggest change in his understanding of women since coming into recovery is that they "experience a lot of oppression." Some men see this and other men do not. Yet every human being knows what it is like to suffer, not feel good enough, and feel powerless. It would seem that this is the place where men need to find compassion for the plight of girls and women in our country and throughout the world. It doesn't mean we are the bad guys or *the problem,* but we can either help to change the oppression of girls and women or perpetuate it. That is the choice every man has. Fighting to end this reality has to be a part of our journey in becoming the best men we can be. As a woman said at one of our trainings, "Men's privilege and white people's privilege are part of the Water." I couldn't agree more.

Nate said, "I have a close relationship with my daughters. I strive to help them become all they can be and to have an equal place in a 'man's world.'" We have to look at what we have internalized and see how it shows up in our lives. I see it all the time with me, if only in how often I still objectify women sexually, as well as in some of the judgments that still come up for me regarding women's intelligence or competence.

If you want to have healthy relationships with the women in your life and you want to help raise your daughters or your friends' and neighbors' daughters or your nieces to be strong, beautiful, intelligent, and powerful women, you have to pay attention to this. All of the men I interviewed with daughters talked about how conscious they were of the fact that their daughters learned from them how to be treated by men. Mark said about his daughter, "She is a dream, and I am always looking for ways to teach her how to be treated by men." I know that how I treat Nancy teaches Grace everything about how men treat women and about the man I am. I will never be perfect, but I pray that Grace will always see a father, even when he is angry or upset, who chooses peace, respect, and love. Ray said this about raising his daughters: "I feel a great responsibility to show them what it is to be an honorable man." Amen.

We, men and women, are both swimming in the Water. To use another slight variation of our analogy, because we have done so much less for men, much of the work that has been done with women (especially in the addiction and recovery field) could be likened to dumping out half of the water in a fish tank. However, to maintain a healthy environment, we have to change ALL of the water.

The bottom-line message of this book is: don't let the Rules rule you. How many men who seem to be grounded in their recovery lose their marriages or other important relationships because they are unable to distance themselves enough from the Rules to show up as authentically and vulnerably as required? Because they were lost and didn't know how to ask for directions? Being a man and being in a healthy relationship are much more about getting the support you need when you run into those uncomfortable spaces, those inevitable times of confusion and discomfort. There is always room for improvement that has the potential for greater love, greater connection, and greater ways of discovering who you are and supporting those you love in discovering who they are.

The Rules have made it harder for us to create and maintain healthy and intimate relationships, but with compassion and support, as well as responsibility, we can succeed. It is time for men to begin standing up and proclaiming our right to healthy and loving relationships. We no longer need to be silent when attention-seeking talk show hosts, wounded and self-righteous women, scared and arrogant men, putative relationship experts, and anyone else implies anything other than that we deserve to love and be loved, and, most importantly, that we are capable of the learning and healing required to bring that about.

In the depths of my active addiction, as a lost and lonely college student, I looked to the Lynyrd Skynyrd song "Simple Man" as the vision of the man I wanted to be. At that time there was nothing simple about my life, and so much has changed since those very dark times. As it is for so many men, for me it truly was darkest before the dawn.

Simple Man
By Ronnie Van Zant and Gary Robert Rossington

Mama told me when I was young
Come sit beside me, my only son
And listen closely to what I say
And if you do this it'll help you some sunny day

Oh take your time don't live too fast
Troubles will come and they will pass
Go find a woman you'll find love
And don't forget son there is someone up above

And be a simple kind of man
Oh be something you love and understand
Baby be a simple kind of man
Oh won't you do this for me son if you can?

Forget your lust for the rich man's gold
All that you need is in your soul
And you can do this, oh baby, if you try
All that I want for you my son is to be satisfied

And be a simple kind of man
Oh be something you love and understand
Baby be a simple kind of man
Oh won't you do this for me son if you can?
Oh yes, I will

Oh don't you worry you'll find yourself
Follow your heart and nothing else
And you can do this, oh baby, if you try
All that I want for you my son is to be satisfied

And be a simple kind of man
Oh be something you love and understand
Baby be a simple kind of man
Oh won't you do this for me son if you can?

Baby be a simple, be a simple man
Oh be something you love and understand
Baby be a simple kind of man

APPENDIX A

Eight Agreements on Males, Trauma, and Addiction Treatment

The following Eight Agreements were developed in May 2013 at the Males, Trauma, and Addiction Summit held in La Quinta, California, as part of the West Coast Symposium on Addictive Disorders. This historic summit marked the first time that professionals in the addiction and recovery field had come together to discuss males' experience of trauma. The group emphasized the importance of more effectively and comprehensively addressing the issue of trauma as a keystone of males' recovery.

In order for professionals to best help males recover and promote a process of healing from trauma, they must understand males' unique issues and needs. This document summarizes key points of agreement reached at the summit. The goal of these agreements is to achieve the most efficacious treatment of males with addictive disorders by urging the field to recognize the importance of comprehensively addressing their trauma. This recognition will lead to the development and implementation of more effective interventions to help maximize the health and recovery of males with addictive disorders and increase the likelihood of their successfully achieving long-term recovery.

1. While progress has been made in the understanding of trauma, there remains a myth that trauma is not a major issue for males.

2. Trauma is a significant issue for males with substance and/or process addictive disorders.

3. Males are biologically and culturally influenced to minimize or deny traumatic life experiences.

4. Addiction treatment has been negatively influenced by cultural myths about males.

5. Males are often assumed to be the perpetrator, which has negatively biased our concepts of trauma and models for addiction treatment, and often results in the retraumatization of males.

6. Male trauma must be assessed and treated throughout the continuum of addiction services.

7. Male-responsive services will improve addiction treatment outcomes.

8. Effective treatment of male trauma will help to interrupt cycles of violence, abuse, neglect, and addiction.

APPENDIX B

The Men of *A Man's Way through Relationships*

I asked each man I interviewed to write a short paragraph about who he is to let you get to know him a little better and to honor these men and their stories.

Bob has been in recovery for twenty-six years. Everything he has in his life, including life itself, has been a miracle provided by his recovery nurtured by the fellowship of AA.

Bobby has been a grateful participant in his own recovery from addiction to alcohol and other drugs for nearly twenty-two years. Despite having nearly lost it all, today he leads a life of joy, abundance, and meaning. None of this would be possible without his twelve-step program, providing a design for living that really works, along with a vital, spiritual experience and an indescribably wonderful sense of belonging in the fellowship of recovery. He remains committed to working through the steps every year, and to both having a sponsor and being a sponsor. Outside his twelve-step fellowship, Bobby has been a member of a men's support group since 2006; he has been engaged both in couples counseling with his wife and in individual therapy since 2010.

Chris has been in recovery for fourteen years. He has gone through some very hard life-changing roadblocks, and has overcome them with the hand and help of his sponsor, his friends, and the fellowship of AA. Some of his biggest triumphs have been being present and sober for the death of his father, as well as pursuing and becoming successful as a full-time artist. He is grateful and loving his path, and excited for that to continue.

David P was in recovery for over forty years before his recent untimely passing. He was blessed with a supportive family and recovery community. His life was enriched by twelve-step programs as he continued his journey of recovery, always looking forward to what the next bend in the road would bring.

David W entered the rooms of recovery in 1989 when he was diagnosed with a chronic medical condition. As an openly gay man he found it very difficult to assimilate into a small-town twelve-step fellowship, where most of the people were heterosexual, and some very homophobic. While he shared their addiction, his history of sexual abuse and rape made him fear the men and distrust the women. The unconditional love from caring men and women helped him surrender and work Step One in 1991. When he had six months clean, the fellowship supported David spiritually and emotionally when he entered a treatment center that specialized in sexual abuse/rape. As a newcomer he stuck around, and some of the homophobic individuals saw the program at work, had a change of heart, and welcomed David into their lives. Today, with two decades of recovery, he continues to go to meetings, participate in sponsorship, work the steps, and be of service. "Oldtimers" told David, "Lost dreams awaken and new possibilities arise," and they have: a promising career, a master's degree, and an extremely loving partner and friend (Chuck).

Earl has over twenty-five years in twelve-step work, largely spent listening to the wisdom coming at him from others across the circle. He is a recovering codependent, still connected to the recovery community, and attends regular meetings. He is living a rich relationship life with his wife, family, and circle of dear friends. Earl anchors his faith with gratitude, and takes time each day to savor the gifts he's been given. He feels profoundly blessed to see many of the program "promises" continue to fulfill themselves in his life.

Ed has forty years in recovery. Recovery began at the age of twenty-one, with little foundational health to call upon from an upbringing full of trouble. All good things that have followed spring from a life built upon the principles of twelve-step recovery, including a restored family, a relationship with a partner of twenty-eight years, and an excitement for more of the abundance life will bring for years to come. His is a story of rewards "beyond my wildest dreams." Moving from powerless to a right-sized powerfulness is the result of healing and moving ahead as the best person he can be for himself and those who love him unconditionally.

Emilio has been in recovery for fourteen years. He chose to save his marriage and family and has come to know a life that he never imagined—a life of self-awareness, service, and gratitude. He bases the quality of his life on the strength of his relationships. First and foremost, he is a family man: a husband, father, son, and brother. His growth is dependent on action, but his key is acceptance.

Gary has been in recovery for alcohol and other drug addiction for over twenty years, and has been in continuous recovery for more than twelve years. He believes his recovery is grounded in the "design for living" as outlined in the Big Book of Alcoholics Anonymous. His recovery has given him a way of living, a day at a time, that has expelled the obsession to drink or use drugs. He currently lives a grateful life through the service of others, the Twelve Steps, and a God of his understanding.

Guy has been in recovery for over thirty-one years. Getting sober and embracing and living the AA program has allowed him to live a life beyond his wildest dreams. It has opened the door for him to live an extraordinary life with fulfilling spiritual, romantic, familial, friendship, and business relationships. The program is also a place of refuge for him during trying times, which are fewer and shorter in duration.

Hugh has been a person in long-term recovery from addiction for more than twenty-seven years and has worked in the treatment field for more than twenty-four years. Some of the biggest blessings for him have been being placed in a position to help others, meeting his wife "in the rooms," and the fact that his two daughters have only ever seen him sober. Hugh is truly grateful to God for the beautiful relationships in his life, and all the amazing opportunities and the spiritual experiences he has been granted as he "trudges the road of happy destiny."

Jim has been living in recovery from alcohol and other drugs since 1999. His life in recovery has been a magnificent adventure. The two greatest spiritual experiences of his recovery have been being present for his father and mother as her battle with multiple sclerosis came to an end, and marrying his husband Peter in May of 2010. Today, his life is filled with gratitude and commotion as they restore an 1890s farmhouse in rural Minnesota along with their two dogs, four cats, and many chickens.

Jose has over ten years of recovery. He is a grateful addict who has been blessed with the opportunity to live two lives in one lifetime. He is married and a father of four beautiful children, and is a good son/ brother, a good friend, and a good employee. He has experienced a shift in the way he values his life and the relationships in it. Today relationships with people, especially men, are about friendship, support, and love instead of opportunity, money, power, or status. This shift in the way Jose experiences life has brought him closer to a God of his understanding. He walks in the spirit of the lessons he has learned, most importantly that he is responsible for how he acts no matter how he feels.

Josh started drinking when he was thirteen years old, and by the age of twenty was asked to leave his family home, and he spent the next seven years on the streets. In 2001, he started his journey in recovery. After many years of suffering with active addiction, he has been able to re-create his life. Living by spiritual principles has allowed him to be a successful member of his community and to maintain a healthy relationship with his wife, and has given him the greatest gift of his life, his daughter.

Larry had that first magical drink at age sixteen and knew in the moment everything would be okay. At age thirty-six he showed up at his parents' home with everything he owned in two bags, knowing that no matter how much he drank, nothing would be okay again. The turning point came with the realization that the light of hope was about to go out. No more recoveries, no more pulling himself out of the disasters he had created. He was taken to his first meeting of AA over twenty-five years ago. Now he would describe his life as a series of opportunities and continued growth. Today he has the privilege of working with those still suffering from their addiction, specializing in treating trauma and addiction in his practice, and providing consultation and training for therapists working in the field of mental health and addiction.

Luke has been in recovery from sexual addiction for over fifteen years. He has experienced many of the miracles promised in the Big Book, some of them before he was halfway through. Some of the biggest blessings for him have been making direct amends with his parents and siblings, his son, and both of his ex-wives. He is currently grateful to be living in a sober marriage and expressing himself creatively and knowing that joy is his friend.

Mark started his recovery journey in 2000. Relationships were always a struggle in his addiction, and getting sober made those problems marginally better. What he realized over time is that as recovery deepens, so does the work you must put into it. Over time and through more mistakes, more pain, and more disappointment came abundant joy and the ability to love in a recovered way. He now has an amazing wife and two beautiful kids who count on him to continue his journey to becoming the man, the husband, and the dad he wants to be. Nature is one of the ways he connects to a Higher Power, and as he plays golf, hikes, paddles, or naps outdoors, he is always reminded to look up.

Marty has been in recovery from addiction for ten years. He is truly grateful for the vital spiritual experience as a result of his total and complete surrender and the contagious fellowship of Alcoholics Anonymous. He lives in Minnesota with his beautiful wife and two stepchildren. He has a renewed relationship with his three grown children and feels blessed to live a life of significance, constantly expecting better things to come.

Mike has been in recovery from addiction for over thirty-five years. He attributes everything of value in his life to the fact that he was given the gift of recovery as a young man and continues to reap the benefits of a sober life. Through active involvement in a twelve-step program and continued participation with his men's group, Mike found the clarity and courage to heal past relationships, and realizes the necessity of ongoing work to protect and enhance what he has been so freely given. Mike is extremely grateful that he met his wife and that his three daughters were born to him in recovery.

Nate has been in recovery from alcoholism and clinical depression for over twenty-seven years. Having entered recovery at the age of twenty-one, he has spent most of his adult life working a twelve-step program. Among the numerous blessings he has obtained from recovery, he was able to attend medical school and is a practicing psychiatrist. He works with adolescents with addictive disorders. He has been married for over twenty years and is the father of two awesome children. He remains very active in the recovery community, where he continues to attend regular meetings and sponsor men in recovery.

Nick has been in recovery from sex addiction for twenty years. He is addicted to sugar and has intermittent periods of health around the issue. He has a wonderful marriage and two boys who are well-adjusted and are living a life that he only hoped for as a kid. His relationship with his father has been healed in his heart, but he still does not communicate with him. He has a relationship with his mom, who is actively in therapy. She has limitations, but they are in each other's lives. His life is better than he dreamed it could have been as a kid due to the Twelve Steps, trauma work in therapy, a wonderful supportive wife, healthy, fun kids, hard work, and some luck; and, because he is a six-foot-seven-inch white male, he got a college scholarship to play basketball.

Okwas lived as a young boy in survival mode, trying to protect himself and his two younger brothers from harm. He was a young man full of rage. At the age of thirty-two in December of 1991, he hit his bottom. He has lost too many family members because of alcohol and other drugs. The deeper part of their deaths is from the effects of the residential schools that attempted to force their assimilation into the dominant culture. He is still with the same beautiful wife as when they were drinking. The Twelve Steps have walked him and his wife through the hell of their drinking past and into a beautiful relationship that at times he still cannot believe.

Randy has been in recovery since 1984. In the beginning stages, he sought out professional counseling and found a therapist who specialized in addiction recovery. He credits this therapist and his twelve-step community for his success. Randy's sponsor drilled the concept of service work into his head, and this began a long history of service work, from meeting chairperson to delegate of the world service conference. His passion for recovery led him to a job in the recovery field. He has been married faithfully since 2001 and has one daughter who was born in 2005.

Ray has been in recovery for over fifteen years. He lost both of his parents to addiction while he was growing up—his mother when he was seven and his father at seventeen. After finding himself in the grip of his own addiction and facing the possibility of a similar fate as his parents, Ray went to the wilderness in search of peace, serenity, and healing. What he found was a life-changing spiritual experience that gave birth to a profound sense of purpose and direction for his life. Since that experience Ray has dedicated his life to helping others find a sense of purpose and meaning in life through a combination of the wilderness and the Twelve Steps. He is the cofounder of a program aimed at helping young men to complete the successful transition to honorable manhood and recovery. Today Ray's sense of purpose and meaning in life are also fulfilled by his wife and four children as they continually inspire him to be a better man and to honor the sacred roles of husband and father.

Ricardo has been in recovery from addiction, trauma, and domestic violence for twenty years. He is the third generation of alcoholism and domestic violence in his family, yet his grandchildren will never know that part of their history; it was stopped with him.

Rod began his recovery journey on February 21, 1978. Shortly before that, as a barely twenty-year-old Cheyenne man, he was waking up to another bleak day and with only watered-down Lysol to drink to keep withdrawal from setting in when he was struck by the thought that *there is no hope for me; this is all I have to look forward to.* By the grace of God and a loving mother who was unrelenting in her prayers for him and her passionate belief in the character of her son, he finally reached out his hand to friends in AA, who pulled him into a fellowship that has continued to save his life, one day at a time. Rod has so much gratitude for a life filled with hope, a loving family, and an intense desire to help the still-suffering alcoholic and addict to find the road to recovery.

Roland is a former drug addict who spent most of his twenties addicted and incarcerated. Roland was devastated as he saw the carnage addiction inflicted on his community. He went into treatment in handcuffs on June 10, 1986 and has not had a drink or other drug since, and has dedicated his life to helping others overcome this disease. Roland has been providing addiction counseling, education, program development, consultations, and interventions in the United States and abroad since 1986. He is an advocate for increasing awareness and best practices related to relapse prevention, men's issues, trauma-informed care, and providing culturally and linguistically appropriate services. Roland is particularly interested in the challenges associated with working with formerly incarcerated clients and men of color.

Sean has been in recovery from addiction and codependency for over sixteen years. He has been amazed by the power the steps and fellowship have had on his life. The blessings he has experienced are many and continue daily. He has learned how to rightly relate to himself, others, and a Higher Power. He is currently grateful to have meaningful work and be expressing himself creatively while knowing that life is sweet.

ADDITIONAL RESOURCES

Besides those listed here, you can find helpful resources at
www.dangriffin.com.

Chapter One: The Man Rules
A Man's Way through the Twelve Steps, Dan Griffin (Center City, MN: Hazelden,
2009).

*The Way of the Superior Man: A Spiritual Guide to Mastering the Challenges of
Women, Work, and Sexual Desire,* David Deida (Louisville, CO: Sounds True,
2004).

Knights Without Armor, Aaron Kipnis (New York, NY: Tarcher, 1991).

Velvet Rage: Overcoming the Pain of Growing Up Gay in a Straight Man's World,
Alan Downs (Boston, MA: Da Capo Press, 2012).

Chapter Two: My Story
The Flying Boy: Healing the Wounded Man, John Lee (Deerfield Beach, FL:
Health Communications, Inc., 1987).

The Flying Boy II: The Journey Continues, John Lee (Deerfield Beach, FL:
Health Communications, Inc., 1991).

The Peaceful Warrior, Dan Millman (Novato, CA: HJ Kramer, 1984).

Becoming Gay: The Journey to Self-Acceptance, Richard Isay (New York, NY:
Henry Holt and Co., 1996).

Behind the Mask: My Double Life in Baseball, Dave Pallone (Iron Mountain, MI:
Double Play Media, LLC, 2012).

Chapter Three: Men, Relationships, and Trauma

Trauma and the Twelve Steps: A Complete Guide For Enhancing Recovery,
Jamie Marich (Cornersburg, OH: Cornersburg Media, 2012).

*Trauma Made Simple: Competencies in Assessment, Treatment and Working with
Survivors,* Jamie Marich (Eau Claire, WI: PESI Publishing and Media, 2014).

*Waking the Tiger: Healing Trauma: The Innate Capacity to Transform Overwhelming
Experiences,* Peter Levine (Berkeley, CA: North Atlantic Books, 1997).

The Trauma Spectrum: Hidden Wounds and Human Resiliency, Robert Scaer
(New York, NY: W.W. Norton and Co., 2005).

Chapter Four: Manly Feelings

Stage II Recovery: Life Beyond Addiction, Earnie Larsen (New York, NY:
HarperOne, 2009).

Twelve Smart Things to Do When the Booze and Drugs Are Gone, Allen Berger
(Center City, MN: Hazeleden, 2010).

Emotional Sobriety: From Relationship Trauma to Resilience and Balance,
Tian Dayton (Deerfield Beach, FL: Health Communications, Inc., 2007).

Chapter Five: Creating Healthy Relationships

How Can I Get through to You: Closing the Intimacy Gap Between Men and Women,
Terrence Real (New York, NY: Scribner, 2003).

Chapter Six: Staying in Healthy Relationships

The New Rules of Marriage: What You Need to Know to Make Love Work,
Terrence Real (New York, NY: Ballantine Books, 2007).

Seven Principles for Making Marriage Work, John Gottman and Nan Silver
(New York, NY: Three Rivers Press, 1999).

Stage II Relationships: Love Beyond Addiction, Earnie Larsen (New York ,NY:
HarperCollins, 1987).

Love Between Men: Enhancing Intimacy and Resolving Conflicts in Gay Relationships,
Rik Isensee (Lincoln, NE: iUniverse, Inc., 2005).

Keeping Mr. Right: The Gay Man's Guide to Lasting Relationships, Kenneth George (Los Angeles, CA: Alyson Books, 2004).

10 Smart Things Gay Men Can Do to Find Real Love, Joe Kort (New York, NY: Magnus Books, 2006).

Chapter Eight: Shame and Vulnerability
Men, Women, and Worthiness: The Experience of Shame and the Power of Being Enough, Brené Brown (Louisville, CO: Sounds True, 2012).

Daring Greatly: How the Courage to Be Vulnerable Transforms the Way We Live, Love, Parent, and Lead, Brené Brown (New York, NY: Gotham Books, 2012).

Healing the Shame That Binds You, John Bradshaw (Deerfield Beach, FL: Health Communications, Inc., 2005).

Chapter Nine: Violence and Abuse
When Good Men Behave Badly: Change Your Behavior, Change Your Relationship, David Wexler (Oakland, CA: New Harbinger Publications, Inc., 2004).

The Macho Paradox: Why Some Men Hurt Women and How All Men Can Help, Jackson Katz (Naperville, IL: Sourcebooks, Inc., 2006).

Men's Work: How to Stop the Violence That Tears Our Lives Apart, Paul Kivel (Center City, MN: Hazelden Publishing, 1992).

Chapter Ten: Sex and Sexuality
The Joy of Sex: The Ultimate Revised Edition, Alex Comfort (New York, NY: Crown Publishers, 2008).

Loving Sex: The Book of Joy and Passion, Laura Berman (London, UK: DK Adult, 2011).

Chapter Eleven: Separating the Men from the Boys
Silent Sons: A Book For and About Men, Robert Ackerman (New York, NY: Fireside, 1993).

228 A MAN'S WAY THROUGH RELATIONSHIPS

It Will Never Happen to Me: Growing Up with Addiction, as Youngsters, Adolescents, Adult (Revised and Expanded), Claudia Black (Bainbridge Island, WA: MAC Publishing, 2001).

Struggle for Intimacy (Adult Children of Alcoholics Series), Janet Geringer Woititz (Deerfield Beack, FL: Health Communications, Inc., 1990).

The ACOA Trauma Syndrome: The Impact of Childhood Pain on Adult Relationships, Tian Dayton (Deerfield Beack, FL: Health Communications, Inc., 2012).

Growing Yourself Back Up, John Lee (New York, NY: Three Rivers Press, 2001).

Chapter Twelve: Codependency

Against the Wall: Men's Reality in a Codependent Culture, Marshall Hardy and James Hough (Center City, MN: Hazelden Publishing, 1991).

Codependence and Detachment: How to Set Boundaries and Make Your Life Your Own, Karen Casey (San Francisco, CA: Conari Press, 2008).

Codependent No More: How to Stop Controlling Others and Start Caring for Yourself, Melody Beattie (Center City, MN: Hazelden Publishing, 1992).

Chapter Thirteen: Healing Trauma

Healing from Trauma: A Survivor's Guide to Understanding Your Symptoms and Reclaiming Your Life, Jasmin Lee Cori (Cambridge, MA: Marlowe and Company, 2007).

Healing Developmental Trauma: How Early Trauma Affects Self-Regulation, Self-Image, and the Capacity for Relationship, Laurence Heller and Aline Lapierre (Berkeley, CA: North Atlantic Books, 2012).

Reclaiming Your Life: The Gay Man's Guide to Recovery from Abuse, Addictions, and Self-defeating Behaviors, Rik Isensee (Lincoln, NE: iUniverse Inc., 2005).